# Poetry Ireland REVIEW 111

*Eagarthóir/Editor*

JOHN F DEANE

© Poetry Ireland Ltd 2013

Poetry Ireland Ltd/Éigse Éireann Teo gratefully acknowledges the assistance of
The Arts Council/An Chomhairle Ealaíon and The Arts Council of Northern Ireland.

LOTTERY FUNDED

---

Poetry Ireland invites individuals and commercial organisations to become
Friends of Poetry Ireland. For more details please contact:

Poetry Ireland Friends Scheme, Poetry Ireland, 32 Kildare St,
Dublin 2, Ireland

or telephone +353 1 6789815; e-mail management@poetryireland.ie

---

FRIENDS:
Joan and Joe McBreen, James Hickey, Desmond Windle, Neville Keery,
Noel and Anne Monahan, Ruth Webster, Maurice Earls, Oliver Marshall,
Mary Shine Thompson, Seán Coyle and Andrew Caldicott

*Poetry Ireland Review* is published quarterly by Poetry Ireland Ltd. The Editor enjoys
complete autonomy in the choice of material published. The contents of this publication
should not be taken to reflect either the views or the policy of the publishers.

ISBN: 1-902121-49-X
ISSN: 0332-2998

ASSISTANT EDITOR: Paul Lenehan (typesetting, proofreading, pre-publication) with the
    assistance of Niamh McKeown, Peter Salisbury and proofreader Orla Higgins
IRISH-LANGUAGE CONSULTANT: Aifric Mac Aodha
DESIGN: Alastair Keady (**www.hexhibit.com**)

Printed in Ireland by **Brunswick Press Ltd**, Unit B2, Bluebell Industrial Estate, D13

# Contents    Poetry Ireland Review III

| | | |
|---|---|---|
| John F Deane | 5 | EDITORIAL |
| Sujata Bhatt | 6 | POPPIES IN TRANSLATION |
| | 8 | A SECRET |
| | II | A DIFFERENT INCARNATION |
| Matthew Sweeney | 15 | CLOUD COMMUNICATION |
| | | |
| Philip McDonagh | 16 | ESSAY: THE AMBASSADORSHIP OF POETRY |
| Philip Coleman | 30 | BUDAPEST BOOKSHOP |
| Gerard Smyth | 33 | POET AND BLACKBIRD |
| Paula Meehan | 34 | A REMEMBRANCE OF MY GRANDFATHER, WATTIE ... |
| Paul Muldoon | 35 | ESSAY: IN MEMORIAM SEAMUS HEANEY |
| James Harpur | 37 | SET TEXT: *PHILOCTETES* |
| Michael Longley | 38 | BOAT |
| | 39 | THE BROIGHTER BOAT |
| | 39 | PSALM |
| Fred Marchant | 40 | FENNEL |
| Neil Jordan | 42 | ESSAY: SEAMUS HEANEY AND THE FOUR FARRELLYS |
| Eavan Boland | 44 | ESSAY: SEAMUS HEANEY |
| Thomas McCarthy | 47 | THE HOPE OF FINDING SOMETHING |
| | | |
| John McAuliffe | 48 | REVIEW: EDMUND SPENSER |
| | 51 | FREELANCE |
| John MacKenna | 53 | ECUMENICS |
| Garth Martens | 54 | INHERITANCE |
| Kate Noakes | 55 | TESSELLATION |
| Kerry Hardie | 56 | BIRD TALK |
| Matthew Geden | 58 | A SIMPLE TWIST OF FATE |
| David Gardiner | 59 | THESE DARK PLACES |
| David Butler | 60 | REVIEW: MATTHEW SWEENEY, CONOR CARVILLE, MARTIN DYAR |
| | 65 | SNOW |
| John Kinsella | 66 | IMAGINE THIS WILD SEA FROM JAM TREE GULLY |
| | 67 | PASTORAL POINTILLISM AT TIM HEALY PASS |
| Jeffrey Alfier | 68 | AVENUE F |
| Matthew Brennan | 69 | PICNIC IN IOWA |
| Rebecca Rogan | 70 | ATTENTION |
| Biljana Scott | 71 | NOTHING TO SEE |
| Daniel Lusk | 72 | SINGING IN THE CAVES AT MITCHELSTOWN |
| Mary Turley-McGrath | 73 | TIME OF WATER |
| Ross Donlon | 74 | GLASS AIR |
| *PIR* Introduction | 75 | INTRODUCING ANDREW HUDGINS |
| | 75 | THE OFFICES |
| | 76 | OUR WARS |

Andrew Hudgins 76    WALKING A TRUE LINE

77    ELEGY FOR MY FATHER, WHO IS NOT DEAD

78    CHRIST AS A GARDENER

79    THE GLASS HAMMER

Philip Coleman 80    REVIEW: DANNIE ABSE

Francis Harvey 83    THE INTERPRETATION OF DREAMS

83    HERON AGAIN

84    THE HOLIDAY HOME

Diane Fahey 85    GARDEN WALK

Peter Carpenter 86    THE WALK OUT

87    FEN BUTCHER

Jacob Agee 88    MORNING MANTIS

Chris Agee 90    NERETVA RESTAURANT

Marianne Burton 91    THE PERSISTENCE OF VISION

Kenneth Steven 92    THE GHOST ORCHID

Eamon Cooke 93    NORTHWEST

Brian Turner 94    THE EUPHRATES WHEEL

Interview 95    INTERVIEW: PADDY BUSHE

Martina Evans 103    DADDY AND MAE WEST

104    THROUGH THE LOOKING GLASS

Geraldine Mitchell 105    BASSO CONTINUO

Allison McVety 106    COATTAILS

Liam Carson 107    REVIEW: LIAM Ó MUIRTHILE

Philip Coleman 111    A YEAR LATER

Billy Ramsell 112    HENRIETTA STREET

Noel Monahan 115    BOG ENERGY

Paula Bohince 116    THE MOOSE

Richard Murphy 117    ESSAY: TRANSGRESSING INTO POETRY

Peter Sirr 134    REVIEW: RICHARD MURPHY

Notes on Contributors 137

## Editorial

I've been saddened to have had to present Seamus Heaney's tribute to Dennis O'Driscoll in one issue of the journal, and to have to present tributes to Seamus Heaney by Paul Muldoon and Eavan Boland in this, subsequent issue. Alongside the death of the much-loved Dardis Clarke, 2013 has been a hard year for poetry in Ireland. The *Review* offers in these pages a short, preliminary section of work in tribute to the late Seamus Heaney, and also includes Matthew Sweeney's fine elegiac poem to Dennis O'Driscoll which missed the last issue but helps here to revive our memory of that loss. The piece by Philip McDonagh, his further thoughts on the art and craft of poetry, entitled 'The Ambassadorship of Poetry', arrived well before Seamus Heaney's death, yet it now appears to me a good way to introduce the tribute section to Heaney. A great deal more will be written in memory of our Nobel laureate whose work and presence amongst us did so much for poetry in this country and indeed around the world.

In 2013 also, Joe Woods ended his thirteen-year successful career as director of Poetry Ireland, and he leaves the organisation in a strong position, having helped in particular to establish the *Review* as one of the most vital in these islands. I'm happy to acknowledge the great work he has done, and equally happy to welcome the new director, Maureen Kennelly, to the helm. Congratulations are also due to Paula Meehan, our latest Ireland Professor of Poetry.

I open this issue of *Poetry Ireland Review* with new poems by Sujata Bhatt, whose new book from Carcanet, *Collected Poems*, has already been making headlines. I'm happy too to end the issue with another extract from Richard Murphy's 'Transgressing into Poetry', which concludes with that final sonnet, 'Knockbrack', and to have Peter Sirr's review of Murphy's *The Pleasure Ground: Poems 1952-2012*.

One of the pleasures of editing this journal has been to introduce poets to a (hopefully) wider audience. In this issue I offer some poems by an American poet who is already widely known in the USA and deserves recognition over here: Andrew Hudgins. And the interview: in this issue it's with Paddy Bushe, a poet very much coming into prominence both in English and in Irish, whose work on behalf of poetry has been exemplary, not only in his own right, but also in promoting the work of others.

It is always gratifying to introduce a new, young and vibrant voice to Irish poetry and especially in this case, with Jacob Agee, whom I've placed next to his father, Chris Agee, whose own poetry prospers alongside his strong work as editor of the journal *Irish Pages*. *Poetry Ireland Review* wishes them both every success.

– John F Deane

Sujata Bhatt

POPPIES IN TRANSLATION
    – for Ioana Ieronim

You tell us how in Romanian,
the wild poppies growing everywhere
are *a living flame of love* –

I imagine a single flame, almost, a wildfire
by the roads, in the fields,
even between the railway tracks
where the sun spills through.

Windswept, they might be, fluttering but confident,
    certain of love and life
as they grow in your poem, in Romanian.

As you speak, I remember those poppies;
as you speak, I imagine their thin, hairy stems
entangled with grass, and can simply feel
the way their wild redness
burns and reels: reckless, reckless with first love –
first sorrow and pain – I can feel
the way light slides through their souls –
I have seen such poppies.
I have seen crêpe de chine, chiffon,
how their sheerest silks glisten in the sun,
bright as fresh blood.

They could be Hindu brides,
ripening in their red saris,
    as they face Agni –
skin glowing gold on gold on gold.

There are days when the poppies know something more.
Days when even in their restless trembling as the wind slaps down,
they ripple with the strength of their ragged petals.
I have seen such poppies:
What you call, *a living flame of love.*
Even their stamens, whorls of black filaments,
ache with love – even their anthers,

powdery and smudged bluish black-violet
        ache with love.

How else to describe their power?

Still, in English, we say we don't know
        about this love.
Do we dare to say
        their intensity is love?
After all, who is the speaker in your poem?
Does she have the authority to make such claims?
What is it about your tone, your cadence,
that doesn't carry over into English?
Granted, we accept the words *fire* and *flame*
to describe something more than colour;
granted, we understand strong emotions,
but adding *love* over here, en passant,
makes us uneasy.

In English, we say the poppies speak to us,
we say their intensity calls out to us –
and we say it's the urgency
of their *call* that moves us.
But why?
Why do we turn them into mouths?
About love we're not certain.
But it could be there, we say.
We can't exclude love,
and yet, we don't want to mention it.
That would be too much:
*a living flame of love,*
or even, *the intensity of the poppies' love* –
No, we say, no.
But the poppies do call us.

## Sujata Bhatt

A SECRET

Sometimes the river smells of cows, of cows and rain –
        or is it the wind that brings
the smell of cows from those fields
            across the river?
The river smells of rain, or is it
        the grass that smells of rain,
or is it the wind that sucked in
the rain and now breathes out
                that muddy smell?

A river so clean, it turns silver
        in the hyacinth light –

Sometimes the light is pale yellow,
pale amber-yellow streaked with white –
That's when the air smells of linden trees
                thick with flowers –
    honey tinged constellations –

June in a northern country,
so north the sun barely sets before it rises again –
A land of trees and dark berries –
Shadows move through green light, skins of souls
                flicker between leaves.
Sometimes the sky looks like milk,
    like whipped cream –

Her child was born into this landscape –
and so the girl's story ripples
        with this northern light.

Sacred, she is to her mother,
            sacred, the nape of her neck,
sacred, her slenderness,
the delicate strength in her hands, sacred
the gold flecked green reflected in her eyes –

There's a path through the wildflowers
       where bees will let you pass –
and there, near the clearing, where the tall grass parts
       is where she likes to play –

But this is another story,
       a quiet story no one tells –
A story full of secrets and silence,
    something each daughter forgets
          to tell her own daughter –
Or else, the mother speaks in whispers,
using other words so the child thinks
          it's only a dream.

And years later, each daughter hides the memory somewhere,
       somewhere – where no one will look.

It's a story that gets lost on the way home,
but the silence burns within the girl's soul.

Sometimes they tell you that what was lost was merely a feather,
or a blue stone the child kept in her pocket –

    But her mother remembers so much more –

It always happens so quickly, where was the time to warn the girl?

Should we say 'warn'? But how can we include calmness,
       happiness – the grace of a swallow's flight
and expect the child to believe it?

And why does her mother
       remember that day with such longing?

The mother blames herself for letting her daughter
       play for so long with the other girls,
for not watching closer, for not seeing the shadows
       slide across the field –

It was hide and seek and then a game of tag:
       'run, run, run, as fast as you can!'
The grass tangled with wildflowers
       as the girls leaped over the softness –

Suddenly, from the distance
one girl sees the light slant above the linden trees
        so they move in a different way,
then, the river flashes another colour,
        deeper, brighter –
                and the wind smells of cows;
    one girl says they were all pointing at her
                and no one understood –
one girl says, 'it's my secret, I won't tell you'.

But her daughter returns, smeared with blood
as if she had cradled a dying bird,
    as if she had stroked its sticky wings,
            its crushed bones –
the redness different from that of seeds or berries.

The daughter cries out for her mother, she runs
        back to her mother who was not really far away –
And as the mother embraces her,
takes her home, washes her with that old gentleness
        as if the girl were a newborn infant again,
she thinks, 'But it's just menstrual blood,
nothing else, thank God.
        Already her first time – so soon' –
The mother gathers words to explain –
And her daughter says, 'don't tell anyone,
        don't tell, please don't tell. It's my secret.'

## Sujata Bhatt

A DIFFERENT INCARNATION

 – A response to an exhibition entitled '*Denken*', ('Thinking'),
     at the Kolumba Museum in Cologne.

The rooms are vast, and some are filled with birds, dead birds –
But we know a few crows are still alive.

Is it a maze or a temple –
     a temple or a prison?

'I ran from wall to wall,'
the prisoner said, 'while the current buzzed
from floor to ceiling. I ran from room to room,
and then, the current latched on to me.'

The rooms are vast and some are filled with stones –
     and some are filled with Time.
The rooms are vast and some are filled with paper –
with Pure Reason –    The rooms are vast
and some are filled with black ink.

    *

Some follow the lotus, some follow the rose
and some follow the Holy Ghost.

While others watch the crow.

And then, there are those who become the lotus
and also become the rose; there are those who can hear
the Holy Ghost speak to crows.

    *

Today, petals wet with rain breathe life into your prayers.
Leaves drink in birdsong, feathers drink in the sun,
and now the birds sing louder, a song praising water.
Everything breathes and all the colours are awake.

Milky white, cream, yellow, green –
a fragrant, windswept green.

If you lose your way, you might find a thicket
where deer hide their young.

Behind you, a trail leads to an orchard.

And look, over there, roses get all the sun.

Pale shades of pink and saffron, then bright red, maroon,
blue – so much blue, and deep violet.

And then, dragonflies – hundreds of dragonflies
dart back and forth –     The air whirrs, electric –
Even the light thrums with sound as it shimmers –
You turn and turn, trying to follow, and see
this garden suddenly veiled in iridescent lace.

Violet shadows fall across a golden light.

Light spills through dragonfly wings,
through those wings, across each lotus –
Light spills through dragonfly wings, across water –
so much water
where all the colours swirl –

And then black, black hiding everywhere,
black moving with sudden leaps –
impatient, this rapid dance of being –

⋆

Shall we listen to the story
about the Dragonfly and the Lotus?
Shall we listen to the story
about the Deer and the Rose?

There's a child standing over there
who remembers such stories –
a girl who watches those flames.

'Who will you be?' she asks.
'Do you want to be the Dragonfly or the Lotus?
The Deer or the Rose?'

Is it really a flame that flowers
  beneath the Holy Ghost,
    a flame the colour of blood?

She says a blood red rose has blossomed
  beneath the Holy Ghost –
petals blown apart by a storm
    we cannot see.

Threads of blood like puppet strings.

'Puppet strings,' the girl repeats,
'*those puppet strings are threads of blood.*'

  ★

There's a sound of bees in the clover, bees in the honeysuckle,
    and a distant, distant sound of bells –

Soft and low as a whispered lullaby, the hum of bees so close –
And gentle, so gentle, the faint chant of bells that spills down
      to us in the valley –

But you won't find the bees and you won't find the bells.
It's a song of the Holy Ghost, a song that will never end.

It's a song that will enchant you, invite you to linger for a while.
'How beautiful!' you'll say. 'Those bells in the distance,
how they mingle with this movement of bees in thick clover.'
Such sweetness and moistness only sharpen the sting.

But soon the bees will begin to sound like machines.
The tune will be wrong and you'll notice a mechanical hiss
while the bells in the distance will ring with pain.

Voices from meadows sticky with blood.
Burnt trees, burnt fruit.
But you thought you heard the sound of bees.

You thought the angels would always return,
you thought good spirits still lived in the trees.

'My soul is scarred!' you'll say. 'Erosion is within me.'

Perhaps only crows have the strength
to live through such a song,
to take such a song into their hearts.
Only crows can understand its hidden beauty.
'It's inhuman!' you'll say. 'It's implacable!
The bees don't really sound like bees anymore.'

And then, you'll turn away in disbelief,
wondering what brought you here –
                you'll feel compelled to flee
from this noise which hurts your ears.
And yet, you'll return to the source of your pain,
wondering if you're mistaken –
The song calls you back, keeps you in thrall –
this tune doesn't change, doesn't bend or swerve
                from its burning brightness.

Is it all a ruse, or simply Truth –
                colder than you had imagined?
The current swirls closer and something answers,
something within your heart, your throat –
Perhaps the bees are wiser, perhaps the bells ring with love –
and it's you who needs to learn their language.

'My soul is scarred!' you'll say.

But you will still listen
        for that was your journey.
It's a song that's unbearable
        but you will still listen.

Matthew Sweeney

CLOUD COMMUNICATION
  i.m. *Dennis O'Driscoll*

You sent me several emails, but I can only find one.
In it you talk about swimming horses, and loaned books
that never come back. You say you won't lend again.

I want to receive another email from you, one that
tells me about where you are. Is Yeats with you?
Is he as mad and pompous as we imagine he'd be?

If you like I won't reply to you. You once told me
that all poets had a word that was key to them,
and that mine was 'border'. I won't take chances.

You could use a pseudonym and come in by junk mail.
You could write it in German – I know you loved Brecht.
You could insert weird fluttery angels and mermaids –

anything quirky to alert me that it's coming from you.
I promise I'll be on the look-out from now. I don't
expect any more of your legendary handwritten cards.

When I read again in Dublin, (if I'm invited back),
I wouldn't mind seeing you there in the audience
clutching a book I've yet to publish that I should sign.

Dennis, let's keep our communication electronic.
I know you weren't too comfortable with this, but
it's our simplest option now. You can attach the odd

posthumous poem (I promise I'll keep it to myself),
and I'd love if you added an audio recording, though I know
this is pushing it. I'd just love to have an email from you.

Philip McDonagh

'THE FUTURE LIES WITH WHAT'S AFFIRMED FROM UNDER':
REFLECTIONS ON THE AMBASSADORSHIP OF POETRY

Lecture delivered at New York University, 2 November 2012.

[Added, September 2013: I first met Seamus Heaney by chance at Patrick
Kavanagh's bench on the canal in 1988 and was able to recite for him
from one of his recent poems ('From the Republic of Conscience'). Even
in that short encounter, his humour and humility, his willingness to give
of himself, and his eye for ways of being helpful, were evident. Over the
years Seamus came to a couple of readings of mine (again, the same
qualities), and we spoke and corresponded a little. On his passing we've
lost an authority 'beyond our poor power to add or detract'. Equally, we
have lost someone dear and close, and we feel that somehow he had much
more to say if only we had found the time to listen. In *Human Chain*
Seamus alludes to a Greek word for the restoration of all things at the
end of time – the one imprint I think I left on his work. Seamus will not
mind if I offer him now another even longer Greek word: *spoudogeloios* –
meaning 'serious-about-truth-and-having-the-capacity-for-laughter'. A
man pre-eminently *spoudogeloios*, a man of Seamus's greatness and good-
ness, holds the affection of all Ireland. There's hope for us yet!]


INTRODUCTION: THE 'AMBASSADORSHIP OF POETRY'
My theme is the ambassadorship of literature and in particular the
ambassadorship of poetry. In this matter I see no dichotomy between
poetry and other forms of literature. Pushkin, Shelley and Yeats wrote
prose works and plays as well as poems. Pushkin is the father of the Russian
novel. Yeats devoted his Nobel lecture to the history of the Abbey Theatre.
    Many poets in many languages have served their countries as
ambassadors. Geoffrey Chaucer represented the King of England; Dante
Alighieri went on a mission to the Pope on behalf of a party interest in
Florence; for Pablo Neruda, George Seferis and Paul Claudel, diplomacy
was a career; the Kennedy administration sent Robert Frost to Moscow.
But I am not going to attempt a historical survey of poets as diplomats. I
am concerned here with the nature of poetry itself.
    The English writer Jeanette Winterson, in a recently published
autobiography, tells us how poetry offered a path to self-respect in the
midst of a repressive home atmosphere: 'A tough life needs a tough
language – and that is what poetry is. That is what literature offers – a
language powerful enough to say how it is. It isn't a hiding place, it's a
finding place.'

This 'finding place' has been affirmed under the most extreme circumstances by Primo Levi at Auschwitz, by Osip Mandelstam and Anna Akhmatova under Stalin. Mandelstam said to his wife Nadezhda, 'Poetry is respected only in this country – people are killed for it.'

Seamus Heaney asserts the relevance of poetry to his own time and place in the sequence of six poems entitled 'Singing School,' in which he reflects on his vocation as a poet:

> Ulster was British, but with no rights on
> The English lyric: all around us, though
> We hadn't named it, the ministry of fear.

I will argue that if poetry is a lifeline in times of difficulty, it is partly because it contradicts the evidence of our defeat. In poetry, an underlying truth can engage with an imposed orthodoxy, perhaps even with blind forces of nature such as the storms we've seen in New York City this week. In the words of Seamus Heaney (which I borrow for the title of my lecture):

> *What looks the strongest has outlived its term:*
> *the future lies with what's affirmed from under.*

Whom or what does the poet represent? What are the poet's credentials? How does poetry disturb surface meaning? To try to answer these questions, I intend to examine the 'poetics', the self-understanding as poets, of three poets in particular: Hesiod, who with Homer stands at the source of western poetry; Osip Mandelstam, who died in the Gulag a twentieth-century martyr to the cause of poetic truth; and my fellow Irishman Seamus Heaney.

Hesiod and Mandelstam 'book-end', as it were, 2,700 years of European civilisation. Ever since the UN Charter became the fundamental document of international law, the future of civilisation has been likely to take shape not only regionally but also in a global context. This potential global civilisation faces uncertainties in relation to many specific issues. It lacks an over-arching system of values: like the Greeks in the age of Socrates, we find it hard to define 'nature' and what is 'natural'. In this perspective, I have chosen Seamus Heaney as my third poet for the purposes of this talk. Seamus is the outstanding example of a poet with a political horizon, a poet surefooted in the public domain.

## HESIOD AND THE MUSES

'Homer and Empedocles,' writes Aristotle, 'have nothing in common except their metre.' This idea that 'there is poetry and poetry', that the mere ability to compose verse does not make a poet, reappears throughout the western tradition. At the very beginning of this tradition, in the works of Hesiod and Homer, what identifies the true poet, the inspired poet, is his relationship to the Muses. Here are some lines from the opening passage of Hesiod's *Theogony*:

> And it was they who once taught Hesiod
> his splendid singing
> as he was shepherding his lambs
> on holy Helikon,
> and these were the first words of all
> the goddesses spoke to me,
> the Muses of Olympia, daughters of Zeus
> of the aegis:
> 'You shepherds of the wilderness, poor fools,
> nothing but bellies,
> we know how to say many false things
> that seem like true sayings,
> but we know also how to speak the truth
> when we wish to ...'

Hesiod's portrayal of the Muses is a detailed and deliberate construction, going beyond what we find elsewhere in the mythology of ancient Greece.

The encounter with the Muses provides Hesiod with the credentials he needs to assume a public role. Without their help, he would be nothing but a simple shepherd. The Muses give him a laurel staff as a sign of status and responsibility. There is a parallel with Moses in the Old Testament. Moses the shepherd encounters God on a mountainside. He fears he is unworthy to be a prophet. The sign of his true calling is a staff.

A second aspect of Hesiod's construct is that the subject matter of primary interest to the Muses is religion and the sacred. The Muses dance by the altar of Zeus. They sing of the gods, celebrating 'Zeus, the holder of the aegis, and Hera his lady of Argos, who treads on golden sandals.' When Hesiod in the *Theogony* and in *Works and Days* turns to personifications of political ideas such as Justice and Good Order, these themes appear as a continuation of the poet's and the Muses' interest in the gods and the origins of the universe. We might almost say: the point of treating any subject in poetry is to bring it into a relationship with the whole of reality and with the divine.

A third major idea in Hesiod concerns our response to poetry. The Muses 'tell of what is, and what is to be, and what was before now' and 'delight the great mind of Zeus.' We too receive joy and consolation from the Muses:

... even

when a man has sorrow fresh
in the troublement of his spirit
and is struck to wonder over the grief
in his heart, the singer,
the servant of the Muses singing
the glories of ancient
men and the blessed gods
who have their homes on Olympus,
makes him presently forget his cares,
he no longer remembers
sorrow, for the gifts of the goddesses
soon turn his thoughts elsewhere.

A fourth major idea is that, through the Muses, poetry is associated with justice. In the introductory section of the *Theogony* Hesiod describes how the Muses bestow their favour on a certain kind of ruler or judge:

... his people
all look in his direction as he judges
their cases
with straight decisions, and,
by an unfaltering declaration
can put a quick and expert end even
to a great quarrel.
[Such rulers]
when the people
have gone astray in assembly
lightly turn back their actions
to the right direction, talking them over
with gentle arguments.
   ... Such is the holy gift the Muses
give to humanity.

To appreciate the originality of this passage, we can compare it to the scene in the *Iliad* in which other hereditary lords, Agamemnon and Odysseus, control the assembly of their troops by manipulation and savage threats.

Hesiod's Muses link together our search for concord in society and the celebration of life in poetry and song – a mixture of concerns similar to what we find in the Hebrew psalms. The Muses' interest in concord was taken seriously in later Greek generations: Solon, the key figure in the emergence of Athenian democracy, profiled himself as a poet; Pythagoras, in his capacity as a political leader, established a Temple of the Muses.

I spent some time recently in the Museum of Natural History. In the section on the origins of mankind, it struck me that many of the criteria distinguishing *homo sapiens* from other hominid species are summed up in the gifts of the Muses: language, awareness of past and future, social organisation, above all artistic creativity.

That in Hesiod there is no necessary conflict between poetry and philosophical reasoning, judgment and emotion, the proven and the personal, leads naturally to a further idea, the fifth on my list of Hesiod's key ideas: the poet does not disappear into another world under the influence of the Muses; poetry is not a form of mania.

The *Odyssey* gives us a picture of a bard at work, carried away as he plays a stringed instrument to a receptive audience: '... a man gazes on a bard whom the gods have taught to sing songs of loveliness to mortals, and whenever he begins to sing they would gladly listen to him forever ...' There is an element of trance, what the Greeks called enthusiasm, *being filled with a god*, in the performance of such a poet. The Greeks were always aware that an emotional state can produce a kind of madness or loss of personal equilibrium. The cult of Dionysus, with which the Athenian drama was associated, could lead to extreme experiences ending in collective hysteria and violence. By contrast, in Hesiod's encounter with the Muses, there is no suggestion of divine possession, shamanism, altered states of consciousness, magic, hysteria, or the use of hallucinogenic drugs.

I find one further fundamental point in Hesiod. The inspiration of the Muses does not remove the need for careful discernment by the poet. 'We know how to say many false things / that seem like true sayings', sing the Muses in the passage quoted above. The fruit of the imagination in Hesiod might be compared to the content of dreams in Homer. When Penelope has a dream that her husband may still be alive, she knows that dreams can be either true or false: they enter either by the gate of horn or the gate of ivory. For both Homer and Hesiod, our subjective awareness of being in possession of the truth is capable of being deceived; the poet's powerful gift of placing human things in the perspective of the divine, of ultimate reality, is capable of being misdirected. This insight prevents poets from turning themselves into an army of tyrants who argue that 'because we are poets, we are always right'. A poem can be checked against criteria that we bring to it from other parts of our lives. Reason operates as a corrective to inspiration. Hesiod's portrayal of the Muses as the daughters of Memory and Zeus – of the human hunger for meaning and a providential god – establishes a channel of communication between poetry and what Heraclitus would later call *logos* – an underlying, unifying explanation of reality capable of being expressed in philosophical terms.

In personifying the source of truth, claiming a personal relationship with that source, and directing his attention outwards, towards the world external to himself, Hesiod establishes both freedom of conscience and a belief in the possibility of creative action. Poetry as understood by Hesiod accompanies the search for explanation and accountability in the community. Hesiod prefigures the Greek *polis* and Greek democracy.

## THE TWENTIETH CENTURY: OSIP MANDELSTAM

I fast-forward now to the twentieth century and Osip Mandelstam's ideas about poetry as they are set out in programmatic articles and in the extraordinary memoir written by his widow Nadezhda thirty years after his death. Mandelstam was conscious of Hesiod's portrait of the Muses. Mandelstam's poem 'Lastochka' ('The Swallow') concerns the difficulty of writing poetry in a time of desolation:

> I have forgotten the word I wanted to say.
> A blind swallow returns to the palace of shadows ...

The following lines are central to the development of the poem:

> How I fear the wailing of the Muses,
> the mist, the ringing, the abyss ...

The 'mist', I would suggest, is the mist of Mount Helicon. The 'abyss' reflects the immensity and uncertainty of the poet's task. The 'ringing' is the pre-verbal awareness that in Mandelstam's account always precedes the writing of a poem.

For Mandelstam, the artist expresses a thing given, something apprehended by the mind before it can be put into words; form and content emerge only gradually. Nadezhda Mandelstam describes her husband's method of composition in several places, for example, in this passage:

> The process of composing verse involves the recollection of something
> that has never before been said, and the search for lost words is an
> attempt to remember what is still to be brought into being ... at last the
> inner music resolves itself into units of meaning: the recollection is
> developed like the image on a photographic plate.

A second aspect of Mandelstam's vision is that a poem, while it begins with what Nadezhda calls a 'ringing in the ears', becomes in the end a statement of truth. Mandelstam's early essay on Chénier, the French poet executed during the Revolution, interprets Chénier's career as a reaction against the loss of a sense of truth: 'the people themselves were terrified by the transparency and emptiness of its values'. Mandelstam devoted another early essay to Pushkin's friend Chaadayev, for whom 'truth was dearer than the Motherland'. In an essay of 1913 devoted to Acmeism, Mandelstam states, 'The consciousness of our rightness is dearer to us than anything else in poetry.'

Mandelstam's overwhelming commitment to the truth is clear. But in what sense is a poem 'true'? The answer lies in the relationship between subject-matter and perspective. In the essay on Acmeism Mandelstam states, 'A work of art attracts the great majority only insofar as it illuminates the artist's world view.' Nadezhda Mandelstam makes the same point in her memoir. She speculates that the measure of a poet's 'authenticity' is the degree to which his words flow from 'a general, integrated view of the world'. It is the absence of this 'wholeness' of vision that separates the person 'who writes verse readily' from a 'real poet'.

Osip Mandelstam's world view or perspective involves a tension between two poles. On the one hand, we have the famous pronouncement that poetry is 'nostalgia for world culture'. Mandelstam had very wide-ranging intellectual interests, including ancient Greek civilisation, Armenia, German poetry, Dante, theology, politics, and several aspects of modern science and philosophy. On the other hand, we have that favourite saying of Nadezhda's, 'A man sits and carves a piece of wood, and out of it comes God.' Mandelstam the humanist wrote out of ordinary life: 'I love this poor earth, because I have not seen another [...] / 'I walk with bearded peasants, a passer-by'. Mandelstam called his first collection *Stone* to emphasise the simplicity of his raw material. How do we reconcile Mandelstam the student of civilisation with the Mandelstam who chooses the humblest of subject-matter and compares poetry to working with stones or in wood?

Let us consider for a moment the alternative Soviet perspective that Mandelstam rejected. Marxist rationalism stood back entirely from certain kinds of questioning. For Karl Marx it was of no practical interest how the world came to exist. Hesiod's questions about the cosmos and humanity were disallowed. The quest for significance in the phenomena of the universe, Mandelstam's 'nostalgia for world culture', these were replaced by selected forms of investigation organised for a socio-economic purpose; the open heaven of Greek philosophical enquiry by a flat roof.

Such a foreshortening of perspective at the macro level – the flatness of the roof – necessarily implies a restriction of vision at the micro level as well. How can one say, 'A man sits and carves a piece of wood, and out of it comes God' if questions about God and the foundation of the world are deemed to have no significance? To prescind from the nature of reality and leave the life of the mind entirely to a scientific methodology produces an inevitable conflict with the values of poetry as Mandelstam understood poetry. This was so even before the terrible crimes committed in Soviet Russia were exposed. For Mandelstam, the possibility of discovering 'finality', glimpses of the world's meaning and purpose, permits us to make the affirmation we make about the micro and vice-versa: the one guarantees the other.

In the poetics of Hesiod and Mandelstam, at least three major ideas are shared. First, poetry is un-biddable and comes to the poet as material requiring careful elaboration. Second, poetry makes a cognitive claim. It enables us to apprehend, or begin to apprehend, reality as a whole. Third, the perspective of the poet as he shuttles between the universal and the particular has ethical implications.

## SEAMUS HEANEY AND THE FUTURE

Seamus Heaney is the outstanding example of a poet with a political horizon, a poet who understands in concrete terms the ethical and social significance of what he is attempting to do.

A number of poems from Heaney's formative period, broadly speaking from 1965 to 1975, are concerned with the process of writing. 'Personal Helicon,' the final poem in *Death of a Naturalist*, alludes in its title to Hesiod's meeting with the Muses. The central poem in Heaney's second collection is 'The Forge'. The 'door into the dark' which gives the collection its title is the door into this forge, where a craftsman works at an anvil: 'an altar / Where he expends himself in shape and music.' 'North' is the title poem of Heaney's fourth collection and can be read as a poetic manifesto:

> Keep your eye clear
> as the bleb of the icicle,
> trust the feel of what nubbed treasure
> your hands have known.

Here, as in 'Personal Helicon' and 'The Forge', the poet is composing in darkness, and what he is looking for is limited in scope and impact: he keeps 'his eye clear' in order to stay true to immediate experience. For Heaney, the modesty of any claim to truth is almost a proof of authenticity, as in the title poem of *The Haw Lantern*:

> The wintry haw is burning out of season,
> crab of the thorn, a small light for small people ...

Heaney's reticence about inspiration and the quietness with which his flame of truth burns do not mean that literature and prophesy have gone their separate ways. Heaney explains in his Nobel lecture of 1995 how a concern for truth transformed his poetic life. 'What I was longing for,' he tells us, 'was not quite stability but an active escape from the quicksand of relativism, a way of crediting poetry without anxiety or apology.' Heaney attributes this way of looking at poetry partly to Osip Mandelstam and Anna Akhmatova:

> Yet there are times when a deeper need enters, when we want the poem to be not only pleasurably right but compellingly wise ... We want what the woman wanted in the prison queue in Leningrad ... asking the poet Anna Akhmatova if she could describe it all, if her art could be equal to it.

To 'credit poetry' is to trust and hope in something that in terms of scientific verification, remains unseen. Another key phrase, 'the poetic truth of the situation', helps explain what Heaney intends by 'crediting poetry' and 'affirming from under'.

'Poetic truth' manifests itself initially in Heaney's choice of subject-matter: the interpersonal, the everyday, the rural world. Such material in itself 'disturbs meanings', in Mandelstam's phrase – disturbs, that is, the artificial meanings of the 'ministry of fear' to which I referred at the beginning.

In addition to protecting a space for the interpersonal, the poet serves justice by addressing political subjects in a spirit of truth-telling. In 'Exposure', the one poem quoted in full in his Nobel lecture, Heaney finds himself:

> Imagining a hero
> On some muddy compound,
> His gift like a slingstone
> Whirled for the desperate.

This quatrain alludes both to Osip Mandelstam, who died on a muddy compound, and to King David. From the Nobel lecture and Heaney's poems themselves, we can derive an 'anatomy' of how the affirmation of poetic truth works in practice.

Professor Ian Robertson of Trinity College, Dublin, currently on sabbatical in New York, describes what he calls the 'power effect', a psychological and even neurological phenomenon according to which the exercise of a certain kind of power tends to reduce our capacity for empathy. Seamus Heaney gives us the antidote. We might call it a 'poem effect'. A poem, as Heaney puts it, persuades the 'vulnerable part of our consciousness of its rightness in spite of the evidence of wrongness all around it'.

In Heaney, the truth-telling poet lives in hope, in a state of expectancy, uncertain whether and how he can be the cause of political change. In *The Cure at Troy*, the 'tidal wave of justice' is not engineered but 'longed for'. The same thought is expressed in a different way in lines (from 'From the Canton of Expectation') which I have always associated with John Hume:

> I yearn ...
> to know there is one among us who never swerved
> from all his instincts told him was right action,
> who stood his ground in the indicative,
> whose boat will lift when the cloudburst happens.

The 'cloudburst' that vindicates the just man is like the 'tidal wave of justice': it happens unpredictably, though in line with the efforts of good men. We might compare the cloudburst and the tidal wave to the lightning in 'From the Republic of Conscience'. Of this 'republic', Heaney writes:

> Fog is a dreaded omen there but lightning
> spells universal good and parents hang
> swaddled infants in trees during thunderstorms.
>
> [...]
>
> At their inauguration, public leaders
> must swear to uphold unwritten law and weep
> to atone for their presumption to hold office –
>
> and to affirm their faith that all life sprang
> from salt in tears which the sky-god wept
> after he dreamt his solitude was endless.

Heaney's hero suffering alone until suddenly assisted by a change in the weather accepts the 'given-ness' of historical change, of the cloudburst. Is there an analogy between the gift of poetry in Hesiod and Mandelstam and the given-ness of political and historical change in Heaney? I think we can answer 'yes' to this question if we look, for example, to Leonard Cohen's 'If It Be Your Will' as an illuminating parallel. In the opening lines, Cohen is uncertain whether his gift of poetry will go on:

> If it be your will
> That I speak no more,
> And my voice be still
> As it was before

By the end of the poem, a prayer for the gift of song has been
assimilated to a prayer for peace:

> If it be your will,
> If there is a choice,
> Let the rivers fill,
> Let the hills rejoice ...

> And draw us near
> And bind us tight,
> All your children here
> In their rags of light

Heaney's concept of 'crediting poetry' offers a more rounded account
than we find in either Hesiod or Mandelstam of how poetic truth
impacts on our practical circumstances.

Therefore, of the three major ideas that Hesiod and Mandelstam have
in common – that poetry is un-biddable, that it has ethical and political
consequences, and that it makes a certain kind of cognitive claim – our
most delicate task in seeking to associate Heaney with the poetics of the
other two, concerns the third point, the accessibility of reality, the
ultimate scope of reason.

### HUNTER-GATHERERS OR PROPHETS OF CIVILISATION?

Seamus Heaney concludes his Nobel lecture on what seems at first
reading a tentative note. Avoiding direct comment on the 'macro' of overall reality, Heaney states that 'we are hunters and gatherers of values'.

This position has one obvious advantage: if we are hunters and
gatherers, no overall theory can dislocate the poet's immediate
perceptions. For the English poet Ted Hughes, who was a good friend of
Heaney, the most important factor in poetry is freedom of response.
Hughes employs the memorable image of a sensitive compass:

> ... the writer who occasionally produces poetry is the very last person to
> venture with his specialised compass needle into the overwhelming
> magnetic field of the church.

But does Heaney mean to say that the search for 'wholeness of vision' is
in itself some kind of overwhelming magnetic field? I doubt this. As we
have seen, the Muses of Hesiod are capable of speaking both true and
false things. Because of this ambivalence, this mistiness in their mode of
operation, the Muses cannot be said to impose a burden of obedience on
either poet or listener, other than the burden of seeking the truth. Nor, I
think, does Mandelstam's 'nostalgia for world culture' jam the airwaves

of inspiration or compromise the poet's relationship to his material. Nostalgia for something, even for world culture, is not the same as an ideology or what has been termed an 'immature synthesis'. I would surmise that Heaney's cautiousness in commenting on the 'big picture' is imposed in part by our historical context. Let me explain this by comparing Heaney to Mandelstam.

The external background to the poems of Mandelstam's maturity is the overwhelming change for the worse brought about by war and revolution. An untitled poem of 1918 has the great refrain:

> Your brother, Petropolis, is dying.

These words are addressed to a star, a 'wandering fire' or 'giant ship' at a terrible height. The point about the 'terrible height' is that the star and what it may stand for is too far away to be of use to human beings. The star is 'transparent', *prozrachnaya*, implying ghostliness, a loss of purchase on reality. Since the star seems not to be efficacious, Mandelstam almost begins to doubt its identity. He ends the poem on a prayer:

> O, if you are a star – Petropolis, your city,
> your brother, Petropolis, is dying.

In calling Petrograd Petropolis, Mandelstam evokes the Greek *polis* and turns his home city into an emblem of civilisation. If it is permissible to imagine the history of a civilisation as following a time-line, Mandelstam sees himself as living at a very late stage, under a drifting or a dying star.

Seamus Heaney's historical context is the sad aftermath of colonialism and the twentieth century world wars. 'The documents of civilisation,' he states in his Nobel lecture, 'have been written in blood and tears ... the inclination is not only not to credit human nature with much constructive potential but not to credit anything too positive in the work of art.' Heaney's Nobel lecture takes nothing for granted about the claims of empire and civilisation. By contrast, beginning with a story about St Kevin of Glendalough, Heaney endorses what he calls our 'love and trust in the good of the indigenous'. This trust should 'encourage us to credit the possibility of a world where respect for the validity of every tradition will issue in the creation and maintenance of a salubrious political space'. The 'crediting' of political possibilities is obviously analogous to the 'crediting' of poetry.

It seems to me that Seamus Heaney's historical standpoint is roughly the following: in the transition from local indigenous cultures to empires and civilisations, it is a matter of historical record that something went wrong; we cannot disclaim the disasters of the twentieth century. We are now living through a period of recollection, returning to sources, looking to our 'haw lanterns.' On the other hand, that we are humbled by our history does not rule out new 'political possibilities'. Heaney's interest in the 'creation and maintenance of a salubrious political space' corresponds to what earlier writers might have called the building of civilisation. At this historical juncture, a poet might not be taken seriously if he claimed like the younger Pushkin to be a prophet whose heart had been replaced by a burning coal; or like Shelley to write in the perspective of 'Love, Beauty, and eternity'; of the 'Power' – Shelley spells this 'Power' with a capital P – 'which enables the poet to make a poem'. Nevertheless, in his own discreet way, Seamus Heaney conceives of directed action in the public sphere. In his own way, he is a prophet.

POETS AND TWENTY-FIRST-CENTURY CIVILISATION
Heaney recognises that the poetry even of 'hunters and gatherers' can be the cause of beneficial change. He describes the 'cultural values and psychic resistances' that eroded the Soviet regime. With colleagues like Derek Mahon and Michael Longley, Heaney personally formulated the 'poetic truth' that helped 'hope and history to rhyme' in the present generation in Ireland. There is nothing in Seamus Heaney's vision to stop us imagining the time-line of history in a new way and hoping for transformations at a global level comparable to the transformation in Ireland on which we continue to work. In a worldwide context we are perhaps at the beginning of an epoch – the epoch of globalisation. If we look to the future in that perspective, might we recover a sense of being 'present at the creation' such as Hesiod enjoyed 2,700 years ago – a sense that we are involved in the 'creation and maintenance of a salubrious political space'?

At this point I want to visit with Socrates on the last day of his life. As we know from Plato, Socrates had composed a hymn to Apollo and some narrative poetry based on Aesop's fables. The scene is described in Seamus Heaney's poem 'A Daylight Art'.

In the death-cell, we join his other disciples in asking Socrates why he has turned to poetry, having never written poems until the final weeks of his life. Socrates replies that all along he has had a dream commanding him to do *mousike*, the work of the Muses. He assumed that philosophy is the greatest kind of *mousike*. But when his execution was postponed thanks to the festival of Apollo, he began to wonder whether the dream was telling him to do *mousike* in its original sense of composing poetry. It is worth looking at the precise words that came to Socrates in his regular dream: *mousiken poiei kai ergazou*. The verb *poiein*, to make or do, is easily understood. The whole phrase is sometimes translated, 'do *mousike* and work at it'. But if that is the right translation, what does the second verb add to the first? Heaney himself renders the whole phrase by a translation of his own, 'practise the art.' This is much better. The second verb, *ergazesthai*, refers to the exercise of virtue or the working of evil: in the gospel of St Matthew, evil men are described as *ergazomenoi ten anomian*, people who in the nature of their activity bring about moral disorder. Similarly in the dream of Socrates the verb *ergazesthai* invites us to focus, not on a product that is made, but on the nature of an activity. The activity in which Socrates engages in the final moments of his life, his poetry, is in itself transformative and a force for good.

Socrates remains calm and compares his composure to that of swans who sing before death, not in mourning but because they are Apollo's birds, prophets with foreknowledge of what lies beyond. Socrates describes himself as a fellow-slave of the swans, consecrated like them to Apollo, and possessing the same *mantike*, or gift of prophesy. In other words, in his capacity as a prophet, as a pathfinder for humanity, Socrates declares the value of poetry. Plato, the founder of political theory yet half in love with poetry, allows us to see that the poets might after all have supported the political leaders in bringing justice to the city.

When everything seems dark, as it did for Primo Levi or Anna Akhmatova, poetry can be a sign of the never-to-be-extinguished alternative. Poetry can be the mode in which our reason brings very disparate subjects, incommensurable subjects, into a single frame of reference. Poetry will not define the future. But by crediting a logic inherent in the heart of situations, crediting the statements implicit in poetry, we find starting points from which to develop our politics.

On today's global time-line – not the short twentieth century but the long twenty-first century – poetry can play the part of *affirming from under*, uniting *mousike* and *logos*, the service of the Muses and discursive reason, much as Hesiod and Homer anticipated the Hellenisation of the Mediterranean – or as Virgil, 'in a voice that seemed weak from long silence', comes to the assistance of Dante in the first canto of the *Divina Commedia*. The 'ambassadorship of poetry', the mission from Mount Helicon to the *polis*, can become a factor for peaceful change.

I leave the last word to Seamus Heaney:

> History says, Don't hope
> On this side of the grave.
> But then, once in a lifetime
> The longed-for tidal wave
> Of justice can rise up,
> And hope and history rhyme.

## Philip Coleman

BUDAPEST BOOKSHOP

*31 August 2013*

I.

Say it again.
Speak across & between

languages.
As he did.

*Ásott.*

Learning to dig
down & over

the border.
Borders

that meant something
& nothing;

who held
opposites,

weighed them
up,

cast,
gathered,

& taught to think
through sound.

Such songs.
The likes of which.

2.

The day after your departure
in a Budapest bookshop:
*Írók Boltja*, Andrássy út 45.

*Ír vagyok*, I say
to the assistant,
asking for your work,

in Hungarian & of course
it is there, *persze*:
*Hűlt Hely*.

Through 'Connemara Stepping Stones',
Rachel Brown's
black & white

cover photo
I touch
words

at once
strange
& familiar.

*Ásott.*

Recognised.
Remembered.
Death's shock halted

by a book.
As it should be.
Whose red-ribbon bookmark

rests between
'The Scribes' ('*A Másolók*')
& 'Sweeney's Return' ('*Sweeney Visszatér*') ...

3.

What does it mean
to live

in words?
To die?

A four-year-old boy
asks your name,

hears it, perhaps,
for the first time,

this morning,
& your voice.

Say it again,
I tell him.

Say it again,
through days dark

& light to come,
say it.

He will be remembered by this.

# Gerard Smyth

## POET AND BLACKBIRD

*– for Sheila Pratschke on the occasion of Seamus Heaney's reading*
*in the* Centre Culturel Irlandais, *Paris, June 2013*

When the poet handed that blackbird glad notes to sing,
it was not a voice from the Blaskets I heard
but the evening chanteuse of the Latin Quarter,
who then lay down exhausted on her high altar
and let the poet get on with his own loved music.

In light that burnished every stone
the sky was clear, the bell was hushed
in praise of the ungovernable tongue.
The stones, though small and easily shuffled,
were stepping stones to lyric utterance.

We were *souls in a flock at twilight*,
our compound a Belle Isle for one night,
finding place-names from home in a foreign corner,
reminders of our *Irlandais*, little whispers
from Elphin and Ossory, Derry and Dublin –

all in praise of the ungovernable tongue.

## Paula Meehan

A REMEMBRANCE OF MY GRANDFATHER, WATTIE,
  WHO TAUGHT ME TO READ AND WRITE
    *– for Seamus Heaney*

Heading towards the Natural History Museum
across the snowy paths of Merrion Square
the city hushed, the park deserted, in a daydream
I look up: a heaving net of branches, leaf-bare
against the pearly sky. There, like a trireme
on an opalescent ocean, or some creature of the upper air
come down to nest, a cargo with a forest meme,
only begotten of gall, of pulp, of page, of leaflight, of feather.
What snagged that book in the high reaches of the oak?
A child let out of school, casting heavenward the dreary yoke?
An eco-installation from an artist of the avant-garde?
Or the book's own deep need to be with kindred –
a rootling cradled again in grandfather's arms,
freed of her history, her spells, her runes, her fading charms?

*– from Painting Rain* (Carcanet Press, 2009)

Paul Muldoon

IN MEMORIAM SEAMUS HEANEY (13 APRIL 1939 – 30 AUGUST 2013)

*This is the text of the tribute delivered by Paul Muldoon at Seamus Heaney's funeral mass in the Church of the Sacred Heart, Donnybrook, Dublin 4 on Monday 2 September 2013*

When I arrived yesterday morning at Belfast International Airport I offered the border official my US Passport. He asked me about what I did in the US. I was a teacher. I taught poetry. He looked at me and said, 'You must be devastated this morning, then.'

Something about the frankness of this response, its unvarnished aspect, reminded me of a phone call I made to the Heaney household one night years ago. Maybe thirty years, now. The phone was answered by one of the boys. Michael, I'm pretty sure. He was a teenager at the time. Having known him since he was a kid I was glad to have a chance to have a chat and hear what he was up to. After a while, Michael ventured, 'I suppose you'll want to speak to head-the-ball?' Not being a parent at the time, I was a little taken aback by the familiarity, perhaps even the over-familiarity, of this nomenclature. Even if Michael didn't call Seamus 'head-the-ball' to his face (which I'm pretty sure he didn't), I realise now that it was a very telling moment. It was a moment that suggested a wonderfully relaxed attitude between father and teenage son, one I now see as highly difficult to establish and maintain.

The Seamus Heaney who was renowned the world over was never a man who took himself too seriously, certainly not with his family and friends. That was all of us, of course. He had, after all, an unparalleled ability to make each of us feel connected not only to him but to one another. We've all spent many years thinking about his poetry. We'll all spend many more years thinking about it. It's the person rather than the poet I'm focusing on today. The person who did everything *con brio*, 'with vigour'. This was, after all, the Seamus Heaney who repurposed Yeats's description of a bronze chariot in his poem 'Who Goes With Fergus?' and referred to his BMW as a 'brazen car'. However the Seamus Heaney we're here to celebrate today might be described, 'brazen' is hardly a word that comes to mind. Anything that smacks of ostentation would be quite inappropriate. As would anything that smacks of meanness of spirit. A word that might come to mind is 'bounteous'. And, while I'm in the realm of the B's, maybe even 'bouncy'.

This last may seem a bit strange but I have a distinct memory of playing football with Seamus, Michael and Christopher somewhere in or around Glanmore. When I say 'football', I need to be clear, particularly when this might well have been back in an era when soccer was perceived as a foreign game. Let's put it like this. This was not a game in which Seamus's talent for heading the ball was ever called on. It was Gaelic football, and I have to tell you that I speak as someone who's been shoulder-charged by Seamus Heaney. He bounced me off like snow off a plough. He rebuffed me. Benignly, though. 'Benign' is another word that comes to mind.

Actually, 'benign' is somewhat inadequate. 'Big-hearted' is coming closer. On the subject of the heart, when Seamus was fitted with a monitored electronic device a few years ago he took an almost unseemly delight in announcing 'Blessed are the pacemakers'. Seamus's big-hearted celebrity attracted other celebrities, of course. Movers and shakers always attract movers and shakers. Was it a young Michael (or a young Christopher, perhaps?), who was introduced to a couple of dinner guests and inquired of each of them in turn, 'What is it you're famous for?' To return to Seamus's capacity to act *con brio*, I don't think I've ever seen another human being, with the possible exception of Usain Bolt, move with such speed and accuracy as did Seamus when he heard the then toddler Catherine-Ann cry out in distress after falling in the yard. He positively sprinted, swept her up in his arms, brought her to a safe place.

It was Seamus Heaney's unparalleled capacity to sweep all of us up in his arms that we're honouring today. Though Seamus helped all of us develop our imaginative powers we may still only imperfectly imagine what Marie is going through. She above all recognises that other great attribute of Seamus Heaney. I'm thinking of his beauty. Today we mourn with Marie and the children, as well as the extended families, the nation, the wide world. We remember the beauty of Seamus Heaney – as a bard and, today, in his being.

# James Harpur

SET TEXT: *PHILOCTETES*
  i.m. *Seamus Heaney*

'You know how your heart lifts when you think of home?'
  – Seamus Heaney, *The Cure at Troy*

At first he seemed so pitiful – cast out
on Lemnos by his shipmates bound for Troy
because his septic foot stank out the boat.
But I grew fond of him, and he of me;
I read at night, he hunted food each day,
and we enjoyed our mutual company.

The seasons changed, but we remained close souls.

Then Neoptolemus arrived to snatch him
away to Troy – I was shaken by his howl

'I need to see my father – take me home!
Do not abandon me, half-starved and rotting.'

They left to join the war; I stayed, alone,

a boarder dreaming of a world beyond,

a small white sail breaking
                  the long horizon.

## Michael Longley

I hope that one day I'll be able to write an adequate elegy for Seamus. In the meantime I offer some brief poetic reflections on my long friendship with him and Marie. At the 2011 Bloomsday conferments at University College Dublin, a number of poets were being given honorary degrees. During the formal lunch Seamus asked me, 'What's the Greek for boat?' In such scholarly company I, who would claim to be a translator of Homer, couldn't remember. I was mortified. Soon afterwards I wrote 'Boat' as a kind of squib to ease my embarrassment, but the poem, I hope, reaches deeper than that. It anticipates Seamus's death (and my own). Marie wrote to tell me it had moved her to tears.

Six months later, having been invited to write a poem about a treasure in the National Museum, I remembered a brooch Marie often wears. It's modelled on the Broighter Boat, one of the most beautiful objects in the world, all sheen and intricacy, delicate as an eggshell. My poem 'The Broighter Boat' is a gift for Marie. Now that Seamus has arrived in Ithaca, I want him to ease aside the stowaway and take his proper place as the 'transubstantial / Imaginary oarsman'.

– an extract from 'Two Boats' (*The Irish Times*, 7 September, 2013)


BOAT
  – *for Seamus*

What's the Greek for boat,
You ask, old friend,
Fellow voyager
Approaching Ithaca –
Oh, flatulent sails,
Wave-winnowing oars,
Shingle-scrunching keel –
But, so close to home,
There's a danger always
Of amnesiac storms,
Waterlogged words.

— *19 July 2011*

THE BROIGHTER BOAT
  *– for Marie*

A friend wears as a brooch
Gold boat, golden oars,
Refinement intensified
Below her breastbone,

Mast, oars, tiller
Hammered thin as ash
Keys, sycamore wings,
Rowlocks whispering,

Her journey's replica
With me a stowaway,
A transubstantial
Imaginary oarsman.

*– 25 January 2012*


PSALM

One wreath had blackberry clusters
Intertwined. Was it a blackbird
Or wren that briefly sang a graveside
Aria, godlike in its way, a psalm?
(He will defend you under his wing.
You will be safe under his feathers.)

*– 5 October, 2013*

Fred Marchant

FENNEL
  – i.m. *Seamus Heaney*

> *The soul yes was murky*
> *and no one could see it.*
>                    – Adélia Prado


Something of the fog has burned off –
something in the high oaks and behind
the sounds of hammers, ignitions –
a shift outward, a quick long view,
to a sliver of the largest bay there is,

*a morning of pinion and stridor.*

Of course, you were not one who
was for the high air and only remote.
You were for the light on the table,
the red gate that needed to be shut,
the irritable dog that hears the world

too much, the scruffy fledgling robin
that lands on the trellis, sizes me up
in the way of its kind, and decides
I am all right, just more evidence
of oddities found among the breathing.

At the end maybe you were thinking
of Whitman and his claim that dying
was luckier than we had supposed.
Or not. *Or not.* Each of us a bee
that hovers over a newly-fallen leaf,

*how lovely the flower I do not know,*
*and where will I enter?*

I remember cresting the ancient hill
at Dunkineely, seeing a blue caravan
in the pasture corner and thinking this

is it, all I will ever know of the soul,
the grass uncut, a land-arm stretching
out to the south. I touch it again here
in the braille of small yellow blooms
I rub between my fingers, pass under
my nose, while a snail, with its horns
of light, works its way down the stem.

Neil Jordan

SEAMUS HEANEY AND THE FOUR FARRELLYS

Many years ago I was invited to a dinner in the Department of Foreign
Affairs attended by Seamus Heaney among others and presided over by
the then Taoiseach, Charles Haughey. It was an extraordinarily grand
affair, managed by Haughey's adviser for the arts, the poet Anthony
Cronin, and the refinement of the food, the wines, indeed the décor of
the room overlooking St Stephen's Green made for an odd contrast with
the general decrepitude and poverty of the city outside (this was the
Eighties, after all.) At a certain point Haughey rose to leave, like a tribal
chieftain, and said his goodbyes and intoned, as perhaps Hugh O'Donnell
or Owen Roe O'Neill would have, that we must continue to enjoy his
(meaning the Department's) hospitality, and if any of us felt moved to
break into song, or verse, we should feel free to do so. (He did say exactly
that). My father had recently died, and I asked Seamus Heaney did he
know a favourite parlour recitation of his, a poem by Percy French, 'The
Four Farrellys'. Seamus gave that genial smile of his and moved the
conversation on, and I felt a bit silly, as if I'd put my foot in it. Percy French,
'Phil The Fluter's Ball', 'Are Ye Right There, Michael'. What was I thinking,
in such august company. So the evening proceeded, and the wine was
drunk and I tried to forget my *faux pas*, and the party was just breaking
up when a voice sounded out, from the end of the table. Heaney's,
reciting Percy French.

> In a small hotel in London I was sitting down to dine,
> When the waiter brought the register and asked if I would sign.
> And as I signed I saw a name that set my heart astir –
> A certain 'Francis Farrelly' had signed the register.

It wasn't what you could call poetry. The bare scansion, the half-worked,
lazy rhyme, the sheer badness of the verse, that could have been written by
Robert Service, or even found on a greeting card. Yet Heaney remembered
it, and kept going. For those who don't know, there were four Francis
Farrellys that could have signed 'the register', one from Leinster, one from
Munster, one from Ulster, one from Connacht. The parlour trick, of
course, is for the reciter to adopt the accent of each province, so the
Cork Francis speaks like Roy Keane, the Derry Francis speaks like Martin
McGuinness, the Dublin one like Mannix Flynn, and when he comes to
Connacht the accent softens into what Americans would call a brogue:

> Oh' if you're that Francis Farrelly, your fortune may be small,
> But I'm thinking – thinking – Francis, that I loved you best of all ...

I'm not sure that Seamus did the accents, but he remembered it, the way a national schoolteacher would have (and my father was a national schoolteacher, blessed or cursed with that kind of memory). And the reason it comes to mind now, is that I was sitting in a restaurant north of Barcelona and asked the company of Catalans, did they, or god forbid, Spain, have a national poet who would be mourned in a similar manner. They couldn't think of an equivalent. Even the question seemed to puzzle them. To read, on the internet, the extraordinary outpouring of grief, memory and mourning, from our president Michael D Higgins, from Bill Clinton, Colum McCann, Bono, Liam Neeson, Colm Tóibín, Paul Muldoon, is to realise the death of Seamus Heaney was a unique, and a uniquely Irish event. An entire country seemed to be patiently waiting in line, to share their memories of the man, his habits, his courtesy, and of course, his poetry. Did the death of Mandelstam, have the same effect in Russia? Of Václav Havel, in the Czech Republic? Tennyson's passing sent an entire nation into mourning, as did Pushkin's. But that was when poetry was part of a national discourse, and when the idea of a poet defining the soul of a people didn't seem ridiculous.

So what was it about Heaney, that struck that chord? And what is it about Ireland, with all of its institutional failures, its troubles, its tribalism, its provincialism, that is decent, even gracious enough to be so moved? The economy collapses, the peace process stutters to a grinding slow march, but when Seamus Heaney dies, people are reminded of something that is uniquely theirs, and that they have always felt was theirs. But what is that thing? It can hardly be a language, since, as Stephen Dedalus says, the language isn't ours: a funnel is called a tundish in Lower Drumcondra. It can't be anything as simple as a commonality of culture. He was born in rural Derry, and is now buried there. But I remember an essay he wrote, or maybe an interview, where he described applying for his first, maybe Southern, passport. When asked to fill in his occupation, he, who had recently quit school teaching, wrote a word that blind Antoine Ó Raifteirí would have recognised: *File*. As in *filíocht*.

Which is why perhaps he remembered every word of that Percy French ballad. And why the fact that he remembered it left me so astonished and so moved.

## Eavan Boland

### SEAMUS HEANEY, 1929-2013

Seamus Heaney's death at the age of 74 is both shocking and premature.
No part of his poetry seemed finished; no aspect of his work looked to
be over. *Human Chain*, his recent volume, for all the mortal undersong
that runs through it, is a book of powerful, vigorous craft, with an
energetic sense of memory. It suggested a way forward, not back. It joined
themes of childhood with a sense of ageing, in a rich, vivid way.

His death brings to a close an exemplary and sometimes unlikely
poetic career. He joined the Irish poetic canon from the North of Ireland;
he entered the British one from another margin. He commanded with
verve and honour a whole range of nuanced responses to the role of the
public poet and the political witness.

But maybe what most defines his work for thousands of readers is
that he was the lyrical Virgilian guide for a bewildered Irish generation.
His words stayed beside them as their island sank into confusion. They
followed his seriously crafted poems through the darkness of a civil
conflict that seemed to threaten, not just civic stability but the humane
purpose of a society. Countless readers inside and outside Ireland who
followed poems like 'Punishment' and 'The Tollund Man' – both of
which are close-ups of the violence – found a language that was adequate
to its moment.

Seamus Heaney was born in 1939 in his family's farmhouse, Mossbawn,
near Castledawson, a few miles from Lough Neagh. It was a rural
landscape and a place of origin: In his own words, 'a one-storey longish,
lowish, thatched and whitewashed house'. In an interview in 2009, his
wife Marie said, 'It's his paradise. His Eden. All he's ever wanted to do is
go back.'

The place names of that region are lovingly braided into his first
books *Death of a Naturalist* and *Door into the Dark*, published 1966 and
1969 respectively. In the final poem of his second book he writes: 'We
have no prairies / To slice a big sun at evening'. For that moment, it
might have looked as if a meditative, gifted pastoral poet was set to
fathom the bleakness and appeal of Irish water landscapes. But the dates
are telling. Within months of the publication of his second book, the
Irish Troubles had begun. Civic strife, hatred, neighbourly violence came
to the small circumference of his six counties. They would remain there
in one form or another for almost thirty years. There was no exemption
for the citizen or the conscientious writer. Seamus Heaney, from being a
committed lyric poet, now became a conscripted one.

In person, he was a warm, informal, self-deprecating man, with a gift for reaching out. He had no time for the hubris all too often associated with poets. In an interview he once remarked: 'When I was an undergraduate [at Queen's, Belfast], I was in the poetry-aspiring business, and I didn't feel confident.' In fact, he published his first poems under the pseudonym 'Incertus'. Maybe because of that old, remembered uncertainty he behaved with a marked kindness and fellow-feeling to the outsider, the shy reader. I remember once in the US meeting a woman – she was not an academic – who was writing something about him. I didn't have a sense it would be published. I wasn't quite sure what its outcome would be. And yet she told me that Seamus Heaney met her frequently to talk about her work, which meant the world to her. There are countless stories like this.

Beyond this geniality, Heaney tended to a forensic self-awareness that suggested both introspection and self-accusation. He knew he had been hurled into a vortex of history; and he was troubled by the responsibility of the charge. His fine and haunting 1975 volume *North* is most remarkable for shifting the poet's stance from witness to participant. What makes this volume and his later work on the Troubles so compelling is the subtle portrayal of a moral twilight in which the political poet can end up working, fielding a lack of certainty into a language of engagement. 'It is difficult at times to repress the thought that history is about as instructive as an abattoir,' he said in his Nobel address. For all that, he persisted in his quest for language and poise, often considering in fine essays the issues of public and political poetry.

Many volumes followed *North*. Just a few are *The Haw Lantern* and *District and Circle* and *Seeing Things*. Each one of them raised the interesting sight, and sometimes the enigma, of a poet who was immensely popular and yet wrote a signature lyric that could be complex, even dark. There is a small comparison here with Robert Frost. Both poets spoke in a vernacular that was enticing to the reader. Both dealt in the lyric magic of familiar things, extending an open invitation to come into a world that could be recognised and shared. Both were capable of tangling that reader in a depth of perception and awareness that was both fierce and unconsoling.

In 1995, he won the Nobel Prize 'for works of lyrical beauty and ethical depth'. Contrary to superstition, he continued to write vigorously and well afterward. His Nobel address, 'Crediting Poetry', is certainly one of the best of recent times, with its conversational grief about what had happened in the North together with a powerful re-statement of the necessity of the art. In it, he describes his journey through upheaval: 'What I was longing for was not quite stability but an active escape from the quicksand of relativism, a way of crediting poetry without anxiety or apology.'

Seamus Heaney will be immensely missed. In Ireland he anchored a public witness to the life of poetry. Outside Ireland he was widely read and cherished. As well as being the poet that he was, he was also the keeper of a poetic conversation that was rich, challenging and generous. To take his living presence out of that conversation is to feel an enormous loss. But it also seems important to note what isn't lost. He was a superb witness to the art of poetry. As a practitioner, he was an extraordinarily fine poet, with a far reach into the seen and unseen life of his country, and beyond it. And that cannot be lost.

– First published in *The New Republic, 30/08/2013*

## Thomas McCarthy

THE HOPE OF FINDING SOMETHING
  i.m. *Seamus Heaney*

What a fool I am to be going into this new bookshop,
Knowing that our poet is dead. The happiness of youth
And all its insatiable dreams, the first book I could afford,
The first kiss, the first breast, the first summer night
To fall asleep with someone in my arms, the first words
She spoke to me were his. She didn't want me to stop

Listening and I didn't want the long summer to stop.
She pointed exactly to where I never wished to go,
Having lately escaped from an oppression of such fields:
I did not wish to return to where I was nothing. So
Adamant was her love for his new books I baulked
At the very thought of attachment. Now I know

The true weight of love, what it's ordinary to know
In a secured home, in a freehold with boundaries –
Back then I couldn't tell. Back then I was too alone
With social resentment, and cut too far adrift,
To catch the subtlety of his bogs and blackberries.
I had missed the ordinary and its tectonic shift

Within Irish life. Strong as Ireland in her makeshift
Tent, she knew words were about her and not about him,
However much she loved his vowel sounds. Sing, sing
Like Ulster, she said, but go and find your own theme.
I saw her by his coffin as it passed. Now that we're cut adrift,
I'll try this bookshop in the hope of finding something.

John McAuliffe

## ELIZABETHAN OUTRIDER

Andrew Hadfield, *Edmund Spenser: A Life* (Oxford University Press, 2013), £25.

The poets of the Elizabethan period are hardly overlooked: Christopher Marlowe, John Donne, Ben Jonson and of course William Shakespeare are now permanent fixtures for biographers, historical figures with whom readers are re-acquainted every few years or, in Shakespeare's case, every few months. Their contemporary Edmund Spenser was celebrated for centuries as England's 'arch-poet' but, unlike his fellow Elizabethans, he is now rarely read. As Andrew Hadfield's new biography, the first for over 50 years, makes clear, this is partly due to the scarcity of archival material. Spenser appears to have risen without trace from London's new merchant class and has left few traces in legal documents and in the city's burgeoning pamphlet and print culture. And, unlike his London-resident peers and perhaps more importantly, Spenser lived in Ireland for almost all his adult life, which Hadfield presents as one reason for the mercurial nature of his recent reputation.

Hadfield's biography is at its best in its collection of whatever material evidence of Spenser's life exists. On his English contexts, the biography convincingly counters prevailing ideas of Spenser as a Court or Protestant poet. Well educated at a progressive London school, Spenser may also have been involved with a Dutch pacifist sect, the Family of Love, in his youth, a speculation which contributes to Hadfield's demolition of other writers' representation of Spenser as an extreme, sectarian Protestant. After a scholarship at Cambridge, he struggled to find work, as did many others who were educated 'above their station', before he eventually found a niche in Elizabeth's Irish wars. He would make three trips back from Ireland, of uncertain duration: to oversee the London publication of the works written in Ireland; to press forward with law cases and to seek patronage from influential court figures; and to draw attention to the problems New English settlers faced in Ireland. On his final trip, he died in Westminster and, after the intervention of patrons, was buried alongside Chaucer in Westminster Abbey, thereby establishing its 'Poets' Corner'.

The other, Irish side of Spenser's life is the liveliest area in recent Spenser studies: it informs accounts of colonial discourse and the entire subsequent history of Irish poetry in English with its tower-dwelling protagonists, violent allegorical fantasies and mythologies of local places.

The paper trail here is, again, sparse, a situation worsened by the destruction of the Public Records Office – now the National Archives – during the Civil War in 1922. Hadfield carefully considers the records. He recounts how Spenser witnessed the massacre of Irish and Italian Catholic forces at Smerwick Harbour near Dingle in 1580 and served as secretary to Lord Grey on his campaigns in Ulster and Connacht. In the aftermath of the Desmond Rebellions, Spenser became an 'undertaker' in the plantation of Munster, settling with his family at Kilcolman Castle in North Cork, writing and rewriting *The Faerie Queene* while incrementally and opportunistically expanding his estate. Hadfield details Spenser's dealings with other planters, with far larger estates, including Walter Raleigh and Richard Boyle, 1st Earl of Cork, who would eventually buy Raleigh's estate and whose relation Elizabeth would become Spenser's second wife.

This is dense biography, 400 pages of text, 200 of endnotes: Hadfield responds to the scarcity of source material by testing every possible nuance of the surviving scraps in order to build up a picture of the world in which Spenser developed. At times readers' patience will be tried by his relative lack of coverage of the poems, and why we might be interested in reading them now, and by his habit of including instead all of his research on, say, Spenser's printer, or his teacher and mentor Gabriel Harvey's relation to Sir Thomas Smith, or in Smith's interest in European architecture. Hadfield's research does yield a complex picture of the poet as colonial civil servant, but his sceptical approach to his source material is sometimes problematic. His prevaricating depiction of Spenser's relation to Walter Raleigh does not quite master its material: Hadfield's contention that Spenser was an outsider – in Ireland as in London – underplays Spenser's relationship with the older Raleigh. Spenser's famous 'Letter to Raleigh' becomes part of the younger poet's ambitious re-invention of himself rather than evidence that the two planter-poets may have read one another their new poems while smoking pipes and overlooking the sea at Youghal. Confusingly, however, the reader is forced to reconsider Hadfield's scepticism about Spenser's friendship with the older and more socially well-connected poet later in the biography when he concedes that Raleigh may have played some part in financing Spenser's burial, in securing Spenser a pension from Elizabeth *and* in finding a reception at court for Spenser's analysis of the plantation.

When he does respond to the poems, Hadfield offers ingenious readings occasionally straining the sense of the poems in his desire to present Spenser's originality and transgressiveness, but fairly establishing that he cannot be understood simply as a polemical anti-Catholic writer or as a court figure. His readings also show why Spenser continues to be mined by writers. Jo Shapcott's recent *Of Mutability* staked a claim to reading Spenser as a poet of change and flux, without reference to his political contexts, but it is his position as castle-dwelling outsider which both appeals to and rankles with Irish writers, and which this biography documents. His castle at Kilcolman has long been a ruin and, as visitors lucky enough to find it will attest, little effort has been made to badge it as a cultural destination. Spenser is usually identified as an outrider of a brutal colonial expedition and later – in his analysis of the plantation strategy in his prose dialogue *A View of the Present State of Ireland* – as an apologist for such ventures. This is a key text for Hadfield's imagination of Spenser and he reads it in light of Spenser's 'history of transgressive publication', noting how his poems offended patrons and powerful aristocrats. Hadfield concludes oddly, however, by suggesting that the arc of Spenser's career may have been influenced as much by his awareness of religious wars in Europe as it was by his actual experience of such wars in Ireland. Despite his own biography's accumulation of evidence to the contrary, he asserts that his Irish experience may not, after all, have impinged much on Spenser's creative consciousness.

W B Yeats, Joyce, the Irish-American Marianne Moore and Beckett have understood this emigrant writer's contrary reactions to his transplanted home, while others – Thomas Kinsella, Seamus Heaney, Robert Welch, Colm Tóibín and most recently Seán Lysaght – have contested and reconsidered the ways in which he forcefully obtained the right to speak of Irish places. This iconoclastic biography is, for the most part, at home with their reflections of Spenser: its uncertainties will inform new debates about Spenser's biographical and historical resonance as well as his poetry's evasive, multiplying allegories.

## John McAuliffe

FREELANCE

That morning, scrabbling away at the ground,
imagine him scratching his head, imagine the thing
as he found it, setting off the illegal, wired-up stick
with its plain metal basin. Nothing important,
he might have said to his father, digging away, don't mind us,
this thing's not nine inches underground, until ... *Now now.*

They shouldn't be here they know, but know
as well the myth (a golden gate half-hidden underground)
and the fact of Ardagh's turning up the other chalice.
They had set out, informally, to unearth *something*,
crossing the bog to the little island, the 'national monument',
where the ruins of the monastery are stuck,

not knowing that morning how much stick
the find would bring. Rubbing peat and muck off it anyhow,
they couldn't have reckoned what the treasure meant,
an open-cast mine for judges digging around
for ways to drive every calf back to its cow, a precedent earthing
the future... When *they* sought a return on the chalice,

worth six million will be the market advice,
the museum reward, by court order, is stuck
at 10k which, at that time, is not nothing
but is no one's idea of a killing. Not when they know
the old church would have remained undisturbed ground,
its interest entirely legendary until they went,

freelance, into the ruins and came out curators by accident.
Before that February morning it seemed the chalice
and its secret index to the roofless grounds,
cutaway bog and unlooted graves would be stuck
on that absurd island on the far side of the bog even now
and that'd be the end of the thing,

its ladle, tray and spun silver stand gone for nothing,
likewise the life's work that would go into each interlaced dent,
experts judging it first *Insular*, then *Viking* or arguing now
about why so few beasts decorate the chalice,
or suggesting a monk, and not a thief, originally stuck
the lot, before he died or was killed, into the honest ground

where it *keeps*, the underfoot chalice, unknown, moot object
of drawn-out legal argument, its undiscovered life struck
off, vanished, imagine, into its proving ground.

John MacKenna

ECUMENICS

They were Church of Ireland,
the girls we fantasised about,
or Presbyterian or Methodist, we couldn't tell the difference.
They lived on farms in the hills above the village that was ours.

Apart from one – the shopkeeper's daughter.
I saw her every day that summer
when I collected my parents' morning paper,
half hoping she'd serve me, terrified she might.

They were driven through the village
every Friday night of that long, hot, hopeless season,
on their way to rugby clubs and cinemas
while we hung around the Laurels, wondering.

At Christmas time,
their boyfriends came from Trinity
and took them off to parties in big houses
at the ends of tree lined drives.

We sat on the bridge at Farrelly's,
immobilised by fear and something else,
a presence that was deeper, darker than the winter night,
an attendance on which I still can't put a name.

## Garth Martens

INHERITANCE

i.
The motor-oil seep of it. The sawdust sheen.
That first forage of his father's garage.

Plucked from a pocket, his toy soldier
sniped among the drill bits,
swiped across horizons from a knot-hole.

He took a slim serrated thing in hand.
*Drop that!* His father
caught his cuff. The blade clattered.

ii.
He didn't shout again. It unnerved him,
how the boy shook silently.

He struck apart the old wood crate,
stays cracking on concrete.
Most landed near his feet. His boy
stole what he could, hid it behind the shed.

iii.
The boy dragged out the great river with a twig.
Erected a gaunt fortress of root, mud and splintered stave.
Named it Belle Rive after his father's.

Aspens withered upright along the bank.
The water's transit cut the soil as it rose,
unsquaring sand, sopping the base so it crumbled.

He could hear the hammer's hook, its reach and wrench.
The crate caved inward with each blow.

iv.
Before the tower sank within itself,
ebbing in the gorged river, he pressed
a toy figure where the earth was soft,
buried it with his fingertip, closed it under dark.

Kate Noakes

TESSELLATION

The best tattoo in a while was half-hidden
under the right t-shirt sleeve
of a jazz fan in the Kloof Street Spar.

He was buying a sandwich lunch,
crisps, a can of fizzy drink.
I stared at his empty jigsaw,

nearly complete, just one tile missing.
His girlfriend, cradling
a two litre carton of juice,

supplied the answer, the last piece
inked on her left arm in the place
that when they stood side by side, fitted.

I wondered if they'd do something greater,
more razzle-dazzle, with those outlines, and later
thought of all his blue girlfriends

in bars, gyms and offices across the city,
looking for brave new men with wit
enough to start their puzzles.

# Kerry Hardie

BIRD TALK

Your dog took my chick, says pigeon.
From your dog's mouth
you prized my unfledged fledgeling,

it flopped and flapped the grass and now its blood
is in my voice. And in your ear,
my call. Insistent, round and sweet.

★

Long ago, says raven,
they told you tales of my kind:
of how we spoke and you followed.

Now ravens drift the rainy sky,
we float
in cloud-forms at the edges of your mind.

★

Autumn's equinox, says swallow;
swings on its ancient tangent,
driving its message through my hollow bones:

be off, be gone, you have no business
with haws
that swell and blood on thinning thorns.

★

I am death, says crow.
I sit on the corpses that lie in the ditches,
I rise up into the wind.

I am so old, I am born old.
The new cut meadow shines in the light.
Already my darkness is picking it over.

★

I am joy, says lark.
A weightless fervour,
a sound that spills and ricochets through space.

I rise like the spirit releasing.
I am in sunlight, wind and doubtful weather.
I crouch in a cat's paw of grass.

## Matthew Geden

A SIMPLE TWIST OF FATE

It seemed as though I were simply
wading into the midnight duck-pond,
green moss growing round my feet,
fish around my thighs, but in actual
fact, and I didn't know it yet,
this was an elaborate courtship
ritual which you laughed at, but
remembered some days later when
the time came to declare an interest,
after a series of chance encounters;
a supermarket, a party, a night class,
all leading up to and back to midnight
and a liquid pool of darkness
swirling like a simple twist of fate.

## David Gardiner

THESE DARK PLACES

I have shown you all my dark places –
rooms where blinds are permanently drawn,
end tables and armoires you simply sense are there.
The smell of lavender and cedar provides small welcome.

Your hands felt what your heart didn't know,
navigating sharp edges and silent spots.
Your hands felt what my heart didn't know –
that the room may fill with light, fill with flowers.

You have seen all of my dark places.
Your having left, I twist the blinds open,
sense the dust unsettled, hear your footsteps
down a hallway that I can't find in the dark

stepping over the broken vase, looking
out, I want to show you that the flowers

continue to bloom on the wooden floor.

David Butler

SINISTER SIMPLICITY

Matthew Sweeney, *Horse Music* (Bloodaxe Books, 2013), £9.95.
Conor Carville, *Harm's Way* (Dedalus Press, 2013), €11.50.
Martin Dyar, *Maiden Names* (Arlen House, 2013), €14.

Outside of medieval stonework, we don't have much of a tradition of
naïve art in this country. Perhaps this is because of a long-standing valori-
sation of craft: the demonstrable skill demanded by the intricacies of the
scriptorium, the uilleann pipe or bardic prosody. To be sure, there is an
equally long counter-tradition of the childish, the humorous, the
incongruous, the bawdy, the scatological and the grotesque that runs
through Irish 'high art' and shares common territory with the naïve. The
literary canon running from Swift and Sterne through Merriman and
Synge to Joyce and Beckett and on to McDonagh, McCabe and
McPherson is unthinkable without this contradictory impulse. Yeats's
Crazy Jane poems, Carson's hallucinatory sequences and much of
Muldoon's verbal high-jinks work a similar, antagonistic vein. Still, no
matter how puerile such intrusions as Swift's Master Bates or Beckett's
Krapp may strike one, we suspect that, finally, they are every bit as
framed by effort and erudition as any childishly executed face staring out
from the Book of Kells. But what of naïve art that makes no pretence
towards cleverness or demonstrable craft?

Such is the effect, and one suspects the aim, of Matthew Sweeney's
tenth collection, *Horse Music*, (a Poetry Book Society recommendation).
One of the first things to strike the reader is the simplicity of both
diction and syntax, many poems opening with lines composed entirely of
monosyllables: 'The boy watched the crow peck at the ground'; 'My
friend used to have fish and chips / five times a week'; 'The sick cow lay
on the wet grass'; 'He woke to find a glass chess set / by his bed'; 'Yes, I
can see you, said the dwarf'. They are lines which might have been lifted
from any children's bedtime book, even when on occasion they move far
from the nursery: 'They blew up my grave last night.' Elsewhere, the
vocabulary has a touch of adolescent sniggering about it, as when 'a
monkey farted', or, in a poem ('How I Was Made 20 Years Younger') that
begins 'It had been years since I'd had a hard-on', we read that 'two days
later I'd a throbbing stonker'. Rhyme and rhythm, where they operate,
tend to do so at an equally 'primitive' pitch: 'A horse neighed a loud hello /
as I went by with wine. / He did it to let me know / he wanted what was
mine.' The phrase 'deceptively simple' frequently tells us more about the

reviewer or critic than the artist, with the implication that if the work continues to look merely simple, it's because, unlike the critic, you simply don't get it. Naïve art strives to be simple without a qualifying adverb.

The poem 'Sausages' is a case in point, and might usefully be contrasted with Conor Carville's 'The Wheelie-Bin' discussed below. Both, to an extent, give an image of the subject in the poem's form, the former ordered like a string of sausages into stanzas of three lines, with the final words of each stanza repeated to open the next. But where Carville's poem is highly wrought, onomatopoeic and linguistically inventive, Sweeney eschews any temptation to mimic the sizzle and spit of a fry-up, still less the screech of a pig being slaughtered. Instead, the poem addresses the sausages directly, remembering the dead pigs 'in each of you' and their ...

> ... hard journey,
> twice, through the mincer to the big bowl
>
> the big bowl where chopped onion joins them,
> also wild thyme, garlic, breadcrumbs, parsley,
> salt, and a good dash of pepper.

The language throughout is astonishingly literal, the poem's only non-literal image a simile rather than a metaphor: 'You lie on the white plate, / coiled, like fat, sleeping worms ...'

Like naïve painting, or fragments of dreams, the poems are difficult to locate. To be sure there are plenty of geographical locations specified, particularly German ones, but they tend to have an effect comparable to the Hamlyn of the pied piper, or the animal musicians of Bremen. Nor, despite their anecdotal openings, do the poems tend to cohere into any obvious narrative point. In the title poem, a visitor from Spain travels to an island where he has heard that the horses speak Irish. They do (or it appears they do, their words being transcribed into English) and as they sing a lament for a red-haired woman the man slips away, head down. In another, a fox encountered in the carriage of an S-bahn (apparently) follows the poet through Potsdam to the Palace of Sanssouci, while in the poem that begins 'They blew up my grave last night', an unattributed voice (the poet's spirit?) cries *What was the point of that?* Interpret at your peril.

How, then, does the collection achieve its undoubted disquieting effect? John McAuliffe, in an *Irish Times* review, writes of it offering a 'terrifying prospect, an alternative universe whose existence seems entirely convincing'. If, taken out of context, individual stanzas or poems seem trite or simplistic, this is because the effect is cumulative. Certain motifs run through the collection (and indeed between Sweeney's collections) – dwarves, meat and its consumption, talking horses, sinister birds, a sleeping-beauty coffin, a fox, a totem pole. As with the bowler hats and burning tubas of the naïve surrealist Rene Magritte, one begins to ask; the same fox? the same totem-pole? One might describe the effect as fugal. If, as the collection's title suggests, Sweeney aspires to the form of music, it is not of the mimetic stamp that Ciaran Carson is noted for. Nevertheless, each recurrence of a crow, a dwarf, a sausage, a ghost or a coffin resounds like a musical motif within the larger oeuvre. It's not, of course, to everyone's taste, but then what art is?

While Conor Carville's début collection, *Harm's Way*, ranges over an imaginative territory as dark, funny and disturbing as Sweeney's, the art by which it does so could scarcely be more distinct. This is at once apparent in the lexical opulence and acoustic accuracy at work throughout the collection. Borges describes the Baroque as that art-form which deliberately sets out to exhaust its own possibilities, and in a marvellous meditation on (of all things) a wheelie-bin, it is as if the poet sets out to exhaust the permutations contained in the word 'flibbertigibbet', which is the literal pivot about which the poem tips. In the stanzas previous to the word we have 'its gibber-flip' that tips the 'baffling ribbet' into 'the lorry's gulp and fillet'; afterwards, what remains is 'the filth that furs its gullet' and, with Heaneyesque bravura, 'the tilth / of swarf and milt impacted'. Not only are we invited to hear the cacophony of 'the rough and tumble / of its drag against the cobbles' ('against' rather than 'over') or, afterwards the 'tacky plastic bill' clacking and battering; there is also a tactile, not to say olfactory immediacy in the 'stogies and bits of string, the livid / slivers of plastic and peel' that have been dislodged from 'the greasy trap of its gob'. Notwithstanding the lowly subject, it's as difficult not to appreciate the poet's sensual delight in this acoustic tour-de-force as it is easy to share in it.

If Carville mobilises the full gamut of linguistic effects latent in an impressively precise vocabulary, his work also sets up wider resonances by literary allusion. The poem 'The Figures', which is located between Southwark and London Bridges, conjures up and quotes indirectly from the opening chapter of Dickens's *Our Mutual Friend*. More obviously perhaps, the poem titled 'Guests of the Nation' not only evokes Frank O'Connor's seminal War of Independence story, but immediately summons Heaney with its opening: 'The tick of two clocks troubles / the air, a net of shadow trawls'. The effect is to animate by association the words 'troubles' and 'shadow', loaded terms during Carville's Armagh childhood. Heaney is again recalled in the poem allusively titled 'Natural History' which closes: 'Our two abandoned bikes / tick in the long grass / at the edge of hearing.' At the edge of hearing, too, is surely the tick, tick of the RUC officer's receding bike of Heaney's 'A Constable Calls'.

But as with Sweeney's collection, the sense of menace is not tied to the historically specific. Sometimes it works as though by *trompe-l'oeil*, as with the final word in 'A horsebox, hearsed, in a copse', where the verb invites us to see an 'r' in the noun. A poem titled 'Hangman', after the children's game, opens in a manner that wouldn't be out of place in Sweeney's *Horse Music*: 'For every letter that you miss, / the pen is moved to make its stroke, / and build the gallows' – for Carville, when he chooses to, can employ simplicity to devastating effect. One of the most impressive poems, 'Didymus', is quite literally haunting, and well worth reproducing in full:

> Between the Folly
> and the Hole-in-the-Wall
>
> a smoker's ghost
> unlatched
>
> the plastic
> catch in her throat
>
> to blow me the ring
> I wear still on my finger.

The poem works brilliantly as an exercise in the minimal, and the choice of the word 'catch' could scarcely be bettered both acoustically and in terms of connotation. But how many more layers of meaning resonate when we recall that Didymus is another name for the doubt-haunted Thomas the Apostle, with the further implication of 'twin'? When he has a mind to be, then, Carville is a master of simplicity. It is a simplicity that is the very antithesis of naïve art, though.

In *Maiden Names*, another impressive début collection (it won the Patrick Kavanagh Award in 2009), Martin Dyar pitches his idiosyncratic vision of a timeless west of Ireland variously along the spectrum running from simplicity to baroque exuberance. 'Rooster', whose polygamous bird might be a contemporary of Chauntecleer in Chaucer's delightful *Nuns' Priest's Tale*, abounds in lively coinages: 'dung accountancy'; 'my emerald mind'; 'their jittery souls'; 'I negate the day with throaty venting'. Again, in 'In There', an exploration of equine maternity which (if memory serves) was a winner of the prestigious Strokestown International Award some years ago, we are offered a 'swollen mare, an animate hillside dolmen', with her alliterative 'soaked oak neck', her 'mane of treacle laces' and 'bulbous inky eyes'. As with Carville the language is tactile and effective.

The book features a Martin Gale image on the cover, and Dyar partakes of something of the rural silences and solitude that haunt Gale's work. 'Independence' centres on a man in his forties whose mother and sisters finally gave up on him as 'doggedly he built his vintage solitude':

> And even in the years when the odd echo
> of his origins could reach him still, in the dawn
> of his middle-age loneliness, he persevered.
> Suicide spoke, but he'd the same deafness ready.

Dyar is good at catching the animal in the human. Here, the man's 'heart, a kind of fox, climbs down to the lake'; elsewhere a mind might 'turn again and lope back to that thick meadow' ('Cult Correspndence'), while each of an unlikely couple ('Margaret and Tony') are lucky to have encountered 'another to bear the hooves of their personality'. None of the poems seems to have been touched in any way by the twenty-first century, and one wonders perhaps if, like 'Sam's father' in the poem 'Equine Therapy', Dyar will remain 'plainly immune to novel interventions'.

*No Poem* (2006) – Nick Miller
mixed media on paper / aluminium composite, 72 x 105 cm

*Territory* (2007) – Nick Miller
mixed media on paper / aluminium composite, 72 x 105 cm

*Child* (2009) – Nick Miller
mixed media on paper / aluminium composite, 72 x 105 cm

*Coastal* (2009) – Nick Miller
mixed media on paper / aluminium composite, 72 x 105 cm

*Amygdala* (2009) – Nick Miller
mixed media on paper / aluminium composite, 72 x 105 cm

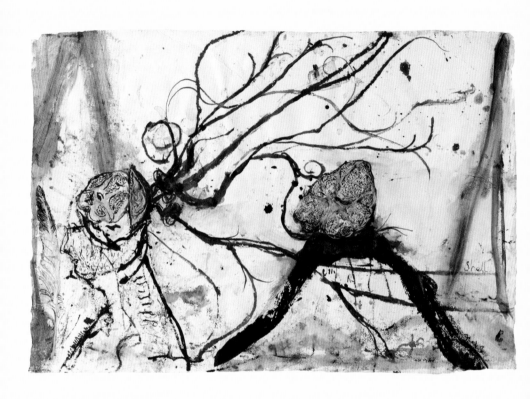

*Shell* (2009) – Nick Miller
mixed media on paper / aluminium composite, 72 x 105 cm

*Mind – hope* (2005) – Nick Miller
mixed media on paper / aluminium composite, 72 x 105 cm

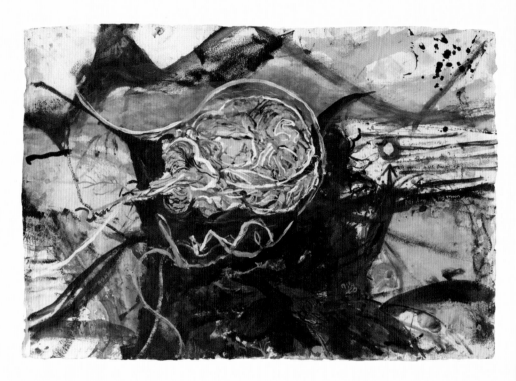

*To the moon* (2010) – Nick Miller
mixed media on paper / aluminium composite, 72 x 105 cm

Nick Miller is a highly regarded painter, based in Co Sligo. Born in 1962, Miller has been a member of Aosdána since 2001. He has exhibited widely in Ireland and internationally, including regular solo exhibitions at Rubicon Gallery, Dublin; OH Projects/Concord Art Association, Concord MA, USA (2011); The Heritage Council, Kilkenny Arts Festival (2011); The New York Studio School (2008); Limerick City Gallery (2008); Centre Culturel Irlandais, Paris (2007); Butler Gallery, Kilkenny Castle (2004); Royal Hibernian Academy, Dublin (2003); and Irish Museum of Modern Art, Dublin (1994).

The work selected for *Poetry Ireland Review* is part of a body of work first exhibited in 'Apertures and Anxieties' in 2011 at the RHA. In contrast to his normal practice where he concentrates on the encounter with the 'other' in portraiture, landscape and object, this extended series of paintings focuses on interior observations of the mind. See **www.nickmiller.ie**

All images courtesy of the artist and Rubicon Gallery, Dublin.

## David Butler

SNOW
*– for M*

Talc creaks underfoot.
It has earthed the light,
bruising the clouds to iodine.
Bandaged cars are labouring up
a road made unfamiliar.
Somewhere, a tree sneezes.

Our scalded hands can't get enough
of compacting cotton.
Breath comes sharp as a newborn's.
This is what new love is:
the world turned upside down;
a slap to the senses.

# John Kinsella

IMAGINE THIS WILD SEA FROM JAM TREE GULLY

I am in a hot room at Jam Tree Gully
Looking out on this wild sea, wind
Battering the double-glazed windows.
Bays and islands, channels and harbours.
A collection of Mizen Head oral histories
Collected by schoolchildren: grandparents
Remembering parents remembering
The many ways of death, closing up house
And dying together, the fever in one bed.
We are having nightmares. The burial pits
Underwrite our assisted passage, our blow-
Back presence. In this hot room at Jam Tree
Gully, I am smelling the cut brittle grass,
Recording the appearance of bearded dragons.
Year after year, a mapping to end all maps,
Picking our way through names imposed
By our gaunt and famished ancestors,
Trying to reset the geography, the compass.
In this hubris, a collage forms and a new,
Wordless book is made. Ink runs before
Words are set, the swell so fierce, swarm
Of wild bees from the storm-damaged tree,
From the quakes resonating across the planet.

## John Kinsella

PASTORAL POINTILLISM AT TIM HEALY PASS

At the high point of the famine road
cutting through the Caha Mountains,
where the white *Mater Dolorosa* thrives
over the slate architecture, the white
of sheep dotted against its transcendent
vision, raddled red heads, raddled
blue rumps, the hybrid red-blue sheep
flashing across the narrow, winding road
to blur the picture into focus. It takes
your breath away and fills your lungs
as clean as they're going to be filled.
In that paradox art is made and has
purpose, but not above all else.
The sheep as quaint as any pastoral
would have them, destined to serve
masters they barely know, following
their brethren from apogee to nadir.

# Jeffrey Alfier

AVENUE F

Streets named after letters march to a map's
measured grid, as if the names of flowers
and women had been spent on the enlightened
symmetry of better neighbourhoods.

This avenue – fated member of the alphabet,
could make us think there were more busted
marriages, dropouts, miscarriages and lost sons
than are found on the streets named beautiful.

Perhaps the houses here, with their high views
of the Pacific's South Bay, are even blotted
by memories of the hushed wake
of unreturned ships and faithless sailors.

The westward reach of the avenue slopes
seaward toward the chokehold of rush hour,
bisecting the moth-flutter of neon at Pat's Place,
where natives and drifters alike, in the faint

rust of exhaustion, touch cold bottles
to sweaty necks, letting the slow scuff
of a summer night lay aside the tired
names of every street they ever needed.

Matthew Brennan

PICNIC IN IOWA

If only we had known that when Manet
Began to paint *Le Déjeuner sur l'herbe*,
An idyll of soft light, breeze, shaded grass,
The wind hadn't breathed for three and a half days,
And the Seine River reeked, a dung-clogged barn.

If only we had known, as we drove through back roads
Bordering farms, watching glare make fence posts
Sweat and blacktop blister like peasants' feet,
Then we'd have kept the romance in the car –
the Pinot Noir, the Brie, the long-stemmed crystal.

Beyond barbed wire, the real thing:
Puddles of tar-black mud and mounds of brush,
The landscape of the long-married, who know,
As Manet knew, that fields like this are studios,
Messy beds, where art ends, and life begins.

Rebecca Rogan

ATTENTION

I'm late for work, but standing in the way
there is a turtle. I stop the car
and bang the road behind him with a stick.
He doesn't turn or startle, but ups his pace
from slow to slightly less slow,
moves steadily toward the ditch.

I forget him until now, at 3 a.m.
when I know he was the best part of the day.
How carelessly I let it pass me by,
the gift of his small presence in the world,
his stately gait, his glossy faceted shell,
his pachyderm feet, his small unblinking eye.

Biljana Scott

NOTHING TO SEE

Paw tracks, bird prints – the origins of script,
some say. When Braille readers lose their skill
the damage is not to tactile centres
but to the back-room of perception.
At St Ninian's and Sandwick, waves draw
then redraw the fine outline of hills
with brush and sand, fading like the braes
I drive through later on the road to Voe,
where three-toed posts – predators
turned prey – escape into the mist.
There's nothing to see at Tingwall
other than a visitor's info board.
Nothing, that is, unless you run your thoughts
over the place names, their tracks and prints.

Daniel Lusk

SINGING IN THE CAVES AT MITCHELSTOWN

That was a death, going there.
That was a dream.
A long way from home.

Long caves beneath County Cork,
serpentine blind alleyways.
These take the place of my worst fears.

What beauty in fresh air, then
to descend into the earth
among drip-sculpted lace, phantasmagorical
elven arms and monks' hoods.

No need for imagining in such a place.
Nor of whispering my song.

This chapel cavernous.
I am the groaning in the mountain,
one voice impotent with so little air
and ancient breath to sing against.

Song like stale driftwood in my mouth.
Dead silence in my ears.
A grave taste on my tongue.

# Mary Turley-McGrath

TIME OF WATER

Think only of white, snow and ice;
its weird transparent grip on skin
as if magnetised for a moment, clings
its cold lust for warm blood, the need
to enter and dissolve elsewhere;
and when the lake froze two years ago,
a young Polish lad slid out across the ice
dragged by two Alsatians on silver chains.

Children in houses near the lake
stood with faces close to window panes,
their mouths like tiny circles, transfixed
by fear in their bellies that the centre-ice
would creak, crack and suck them down
to where torpid glass-eyed pike eased by.

## Ross Donlon

GLASS AIR
  *– for Susan Mannion*

We're chatting in the kitchen at Annaghmakerrig
when there's a sudden flurry outside the window –

a pair of green finches are a whirling burst
of chase mating or tumbling in a birdfight.

But one, the more distracted by excitement,
or deceived that both images of sky are real,

discovers too late that air is suddenly glass,
that nothing is suddenly something hard.

It's a polite bump in our conversation
which we all hear, look up – inside to out –

to see the bird still and quiet. Someone notices
nothing – no heartbeat or bird's eye quiver.

The partner or rival (partner surely) flits and
flickers but at one remove, as though a second

force keeps the bird away from the window.
One of us asks should we bring it in or wait

for it to wake. But too many minutes go by
as it stares into the garden and only rain

moves its feathers. Later Susan carries it
out of sight but we sense its tiny heaviness,

a chance audience to a mortality play
seen through our own reflections.

# INTRODUCING ANDREW HUDGINS

The work of Andrew Hudgins is alive with intelligence and grace. There is an oddness that is attractive, alongside a lyric strength that is formidable. There is humour alongside deeply serious awareness of the difficulties of our life on earth. Rita Dove wrote, 'Andrew Hudgins is a natural storyteller. The surfaces of his poems – their quirky economy, the sheer music of his prosody – are so right because they go so deep.' Hudgins is the author of many books of poems, including *Saints and Strangers*, *The Glass Hammer*, and most recently *A Clown at Midnight*. He has been a finalist for the National Book Award and the Pulitzer Prize, is a recipient of Guggenheim and National Endowment for the Arts fellowships, as well as the Harper Lee Award. He has published a quirky and delightful memoir, *The Joker*, and currently teaches in the Department of English at Ohio State University.

## THE OFFICES

Whether we have slept
through Matins' dream offices
or lain awake, we rise
to a morning bell we do not
call Lauds, and not calling it
Ablution, we, for the day's
offices, flush dust
and dead skin from our many
creases. On the highway
and at computers pinging all day
with the needs and even dreams
of those to whom we minister,
we labour at gratitude through long
and exhausting offices
we do not call Terces, Sexts,
and Nones. At Vespers we share
without bodies a meal not
exactly a Eucharist,
and before the Compline bell's
imagined ringing, we
indulge in bourbon, sex,
or prayer, and then lie down,
thankful for tomorrow's impossible

offices, apostles prospering
somehow under the Lord's
preposterous auspices.


OUR WARS

Curled in curled folders, the last reports
were filed by hands infirm now
or gone. Months, even years
go by without our reading
of recovered bones and bits of brass
that shone once on the raked,
immaculate parade grounds of another age.
Our current wars and our current dead
are the headlines. Shelves fill with books
explaining in cool and novel ways
the wars of our youth, but the immense
granite memorials saying 'We will never forget'
and 'We will always remember' echo
only with the tactful murmuring of caretakers.
The living veterans are too frail to visit,
even the widows are vanishing, and the young
grieve by granite engraved yesterday.


     – 'The Offices' and 'Our Wars' are taken from *A Clown at*
       *Midnight* (Mariner Books, 2013)


WALKING A TRUE LINE

Red lights whirling behind her in the sun,
a cop ordered me off the trestle. *Why?*
I asked, squinting. I knew what she'd say.
I loved this shortcut to my bad job, loved walking
above the street and then above the river,
mincing across the slick, splintering ties
– a true line against a hard blue sky –
teasing a fear of heights with a love of rivers.

*The trains don't use it anymore*, I called
down to the voice that yelled what authority
must yell: 'Get down anyway!' What
a surety the State was – Mom, with a holstered
nine millimetre.
                        That evening, as I trudged,
obeisant, below the trestle, giving Mom
time to forget, the creosoted posts,
oozing tar, shuddered like oracles.
Above, unseen, a lugubrious chugging mass
passed over, painstakingly, almost half aware,
as gods proceed when they think they love us,
we who are in this world to be swept away.


ELEGY FOR MY FATHER, WHO IS NOT DEAD

One day I'll lift the telephone
and be told my father's dead. He's ready.
In the sureness of his faith, he talks
about the world beyond this world
as though his reservations have
been made. I think he wants to go,
a little bit – a new desire
to travel building up, an itch
to see fresh worlds. Or older ones.
He thinks that when I follow him
he'll wrap me in his arms and laugh,
the way he did when I arrived
on earth. I do not think he's right.
He's ready. I am not. I can't
just say goodbye as cheerfully
as if he were embarking on a trip
to make my later trip go well.
I see myself on deck, convinced
his ship's gone down, while he's convinced
I'll see him standing on the dock
and waving, shouting, *Welcome back*.

CHRIST AS A GARDENER

The boxwoods planted in the park spell LIVE.
I never noticed it until they died.
Before, the entwined green had smudged the word
unreadable. And when they take their own advice
again – come spring, come Easter – no one will know
a word is buried in the leaves. I love
that Mary thought her resurrected Lord
a gardener. It wasn't just the broad-brimmed hat
and muddy robe that fooled her: he was that changed.
He looks across the unturned field, the riot
of unscythed grass, the smattering of wildflowers.
Before he can stop himself, he's on his knees.
He roots up stubborn weeds, pinches the suckers,
deciding order here – what lives, what dies,
and how. But it goes deeper even than that.
His hands burn and his bare feet smoulder. He longs
to lie down inside the long, dew-moist furrows
and press his pierced side and his broken forehead
into the dirt. But he's already done it –
passed through one death and out the other side.
He laughs. He kicks his bright spade in the earth
and turns it over. Spring flashes by, then harvest.
Beneath his feet, seeds dance into the air.
They rise, and he, not noticing, ascends
on midair steppingstones of dandelion,
of milkweed, thistle, cattail, and goldenrod.

THE GLASS HAMMER

My mother's knickknack crystal hammer
shone on the shelf. 'Put that thing down.
It's not a play-pretty.' Tap, tap
against my wooden blocks. 'I said,
PUT THAT THING DOWN!'

But when she wasn't looking – ha! –
I'd sneak back to the hammer, and heft it.
Enchanted, I held it to my eyes
and watched, through it, the living room
shift, waver, and go shimmery – haloed

with hidden fire. Our worn green sofa glowed
and lost its shape, as if some deeper shape
were trying to break loose. The chairs,
the walls, the cross-stitched pictures all
let go, smeared into one another.

I scrounged a rust-flecked nail, and hit it.
The hammer shattered in my hand.
Blood spattered on my shorts. I screamed,
was snatched off my fat bloody feet,
rushed to the doctor, stitched, cooed at, spanked,

embraced, told *never, never, never,*
*do that again*, and pondered how
I could, the hammer having burst,
and not, therefore, a proper hammer
despite the gorgeous world it held.


– 'Walking a True Line', 'Elegy For My Father, Who Is Not Dead',
  'Christ as a Gardener' and 'The Glass Hammer' are taken from
  *American Rendering: New and Selected Poems* (Houghton Mifflin
  Harcourt, 2010)

Philip Coleman

## THE POSSIBILITIES OF WHAT HAPPENS NEXT

Dannie Abse, *Speak, Old Parrot* (Hutchinson, 2013), £12.

> With 'Speke, Parott, I pray yow,' full curteslye they sey,
> 'Parott ys a goodlye byrde and a pratye popagay.'

Thus John Skelton (1460-1529), tutor to the young Henry VIII, self-styled Poet Laureate, and author of a number of important political and satirical poems including *The Bowge of Court* (1499) and *Colyn Cloute* (1522). Skelton's *Speke, Parott*, written in 1521, is a long and difficult work in which many of the early modern poet's formal and metrical skills are displayed. He is perhaps best known today as the inventor of 'Skeltonics', a verse form defined in the *Oxford English Dictionary* as 'consisting of short irregular lines with frequent running on of the same rhyme', not unlike what one finds in the lyrics of contemporary rap artists such as Snoop Dogg or Tupac Shakur. Dogg and Shakur may not feature in Dannie Abse's poems, but *Speak, Old Parrot* engages with many other figures throughout the history of poetry, including Skelton, from the fourteenth-century Welsh poet Dafydd ap Gwilym ('The Summer Frustrations of Dafydd ap Gwilym') to Robert Browning (from whom the book's epigraph is taken), Thomas Hardy and W B Yeats ('Talking to Myself'), Frank O'Hara ('Perspectives'), and Rainer Maria Rilke ('Rilke's Confession'). In addition to the poets there are references in *Speak, Old Parrot* to composers (Beethoven, Mozart, Smetena, Wagner) and prose writers (Primo Levi), giving an overall impression of Abse as a poet of deep learning and broad cultural interests. This is as one might expect of a poet who is also a former President of the Poetry Society and the author of over thirty books of poetry, fiction, memoir, plays, and criticism. In 2012 he was awarded a CBE for his Services to Poetry and Literature.

Like Skelton, however, and Dogg or Shakur for that matter, Abse is not afraid to cast a cynical eye on the world around him. At least four of the poems in *Speak, Old Parrot* are set in a café called L'artista – 'Parrotscold', 'Perspectives', 'Pre-Xmas at L'artista' and 'Wasp' – and this positioning of the poet in a public space affords interesting viewpoints. Whether 'L'artista' is real or imagined is insignificant. The point is that it dramatises the figure of the poet as a shrewd observer of social reality, from the 'small / world's wounds' that trouble the speaker of 'Parrotscold' as he contemplates a dead lover's absence, to the transformation into 'a little, loud, nazi-insect official' of a wasp in the poem of that title. While many of the poems in *Speak, Old Parrot* dwell on the experience of time, ageing, and memory – Abse was born in 1923 – his poems are troubled by a real sense of history repeating itself, what he calls 'The shock of the Old!' in 'Side Effects'. There is always a strong suggestion of the personal in Abse's work: many of the poems in this book seem to reflect not only on the loss of the poet's wife, Joan, who died in a car crash in 2005, but also on the deaths of friends and other family members – as in 'Portrait of an Old Doctor', for example, and 'Moonbright' – but he is also a poet whose work offers new perspectives on the contemporary social, cultural and political environment, from Wales (in 'The Bus') to Turkey (in 'Cats') and beyond.

In 'A Fan' Abse satirises the reader whose 'first sedative gust of praise turned / into an imperious fountain'. There is a great deal to praise in *Speak, Old Parrot*, however, and Abse's deft handling of personal and public subject matter, without ever allowing one to overwhelm the other, is one of the great strengths of this book. That, and his formal skill, whether he is recreating the voice of Dafydd Ap Gwilym in twenty-first century colloquial English ('Then whoops! Zips of Sabbath-scolding light / bullied the heights above Cardigan Bay') or considering Wagner as a 'Genius with the soul of a vulture' ('Wagner'). His 'Fan' may point out 'nuances' the poet 'didn't intend', but the poems of *Speak, Old Parrot* are thematically and formally various, inviting a wide variety of responses and, perhaps, readerships. Abse's publishers, Hutchinson, also deserve credit for doing such a beautiful job with the print and design of this collection. It is worth pointing out, indeed, that Hutchinson has been true to Abse and his work from the very beginning of his publishing career: he published his first collection with them in the 1940s.

In the opening poem of *Speak, Old Parrot* ('Talking to Myself'), Abse writes of 'the mildew of age' where 'all pavements slope uphill // slow slow / toward an exit'. 'Quick, quick / speak, old parrot, / do I not feed you with my life?' the poem concludes, and the collection as a whole seems to offer a tentative answer to this question in the following lines:

> Sometimes you choired loudly, dionysiac
> (the drama of an exclamation mark!)
> and sometimes you word-whispered sedately.
>
> Now I'm tired and you nest elsewhere.
> Bird, your cage is empty. Will you come back?
> I see no feathers in the wind.

There is plenty of the 'dionysiac' in the poems of *Speak, Old Parrot*, and the melancholy note of these lines is complicated by the spirit of play and worldly open-mindedness that is in evidence elsewhere in the collection, as it is throughout Abse's work. Whether Abse publishes another collection of poems in his lifetime or not is irrelevant. These poems, together with those gathered in his many other books, will continue to 'come back' and engage readers for years to come. '*Crescet in immensum me vivo Psittacus iste; / Hinc mea dicetur Skeltonidis inclita fama*', John Skelton wrote at the end of *Speke, Parott*: 'This parrot will grow immensely in my lifetime; / Hence the glorious fame of me, Skelton, will be celebrated.' 'Wide awake or half asleep you liked to be / deceptive', Abse writes in 'Gone?', 'yet never babblative enough / to employ the bald serious scholars.' Abse's bird may 'nest elsewhere' but the unmistakable music of its song should sound clearly wherever contemporary poetry is read and appreciated.

## Francis Harvey

### THE INTERPRETATION OF DREAMS

On one of those dove-grey
Yeatsian sort of days
we often have around here
I had only to think
of the gait of that seal
now asleep on the strand
to know it was dreaming
about the walk of a queen.


### HERON AGAIN

If you wish to know the shape
that distant heron makes
standing on its stony plinth
in the gathering dark
you must allow me
to finish this poem
not with a full stop
but with this exclamation mark!

Francis Harvey

He missed the fire in the hearth,
the rustle of mice in the thatch,
and the way the flagged kitchen floor,
faithful to the lie of the land,
sloped down to the draughty gap of the door.
Now he had to make do with the hiss
of the gas and the fusillades
of rain and hail on the corrugated roof.
When the light failed he'd get out the candle.
He liked watching the shadows dancing
on the walls; it reminded him of the past:
the crackle and spit of wood, the stir
collapsing sods of turf used to make in the hearth.
When the dog died he didn't get another.
What would a crippled old man
with no sheep want with a dog?
Every time he hobbled out through his door
he had to face what was left of the old house
starting bit by bit to incorporate
itself into the landscape again:
a whinbush poking through the bedroom window,
grass enough to make a cock of hay
growing out of the sagging thatch.
And then there was the mountain waiting
to reclaim the few acres he and his father
had wrested from it with not much more than
a spade and a scythe and their bare hands.
It was a holiday home the man
from the council had said, we've brought you
a holiday home all the way from Bundoran
and he'd thought of how his mother
had once bought him a stick of Bundoran rock
on a day trip there years ago.

## Diane Fahey

GARDEN WALK
  *– in memory of my mother*

A stand of ivory irises, gold-tongued,
cinerarias in royal velvets.
We pass my father's camellia tree,
its yield of coral cups the first since his death.
Long years. You call it 'the miracle tree'.
Nearby, this mandala bloom: splayed petals
frame the abounding heart, heart-red.

I think of these hopeful, circumspect days
as your harvest won from pain endured;
this garden your own small share
of life's quest for beauty in survival.
At dusk, whether we listen or not,
bird songs will wreathe this old house in splendour.
Later, lotus-stars on a black pond.

## Peter Carpenter

THE WALK OUT
 *– for Peter Robinson at sixty*

The very last of October and blackberries
still there, edible, past barbed wire coiling
from fence-posts in diminishing concentrics
and it's cumulus that's built up its case
over an old haunt, the beach at Walberswick.
We are left to imagine it – the tide angling
into gradations of pebbles, staggered groynes.
Verticals in flat-lands play such funny tricks

so let's keep our heads down, take in bracken,
its fish-spine patterns, ivy over flint, hacked-at
nettles spring-green, resurgent, a sign for 'loose
recyclables only'. On this 'characteristic' open
heath we might catch silver studded blue butterflies,
and, later on, there's the strong chance of stargazing.

Peter Carpenter

Some days he has to mince fog. He flops its coils
across the chopping-board fens where water
flashes up its big knives. Birds that once rose into air
he hangs now from stainless steel hooks on a rail,

plumage indicative of lost motion – the flap
of pheasant or teal beaten out for the gun.
Sky-lines are cleavered then put through the slicer;
stratus-rind come dawn, fat-ribbon then darker stuff –

stormcloud markings with rainbow potential.
His fingers are the putty smuts of fires that have been
smouldering all week over bundled faggots. Spires
dating from the wool trade are distant pencil stubs for him

to scribble out sums on grease-proof sheets.
Shoulder, knuckle, trotters, belly, lights. The dripping air.
Nowadays it's hard to see past such a corpse-terrain.
Each night, out the back, he hoses down marble and stone.

Jacob Agee

MORNING MANTIS

The soft stillness of the *polje*
Beneath the cool sea-blue sky,
Its beautiful oceanic vacancy perforated
By a stream of vapour
Left by a shiny plane
Listing through the immense blue.
Morning sublimity.
The smell of fresh coffee
Floats in gentle light drafts through the air to me
And the rich creamy taste of fresh milk in my mouth.
Above me, on the ridge of the roof,
The martins mass for their morning gossip.
Perched there, in exquisite African beauty
Of pied feathers, hazelnut brown and black,
Heads up, breasts out like generals,
They blast out their fantastic tongue of twerps,
Chirps, stutters, and twisted mutters.

Below me, on the porch, the kitten.
Snow white with a braided tail of ginger
And hazelnut and with dappled feet of browns,
With steel blue eyes and a tricksy bat-like face
And an expression of infantile intrigue,
She plays. She sits in the grass and I can see
How small she is. The green blades engulf
Her white form, and tower over her flexed ears,
And I can see the comfort a cat has in grass.
She rolls on her back, climbs the stone bench,
The table leg, and my leg. She stares transfixed
At flowers. She meows squeakishly, climbs into
My sandal, stretches, yawns.
She chases shadows, watching them intensely, creeping,
Then pouncing with her tiny paw, bewildered
That the shadows always flit away out of her reach.

I can see her learning as she stares
With her intense eyes, strategising
Her next capture of a shadow or her next climb.
And I am learning: I see her feline child's wisdom
And praise it, and I feel like an Egyptian in her presence.

*Then*, the shrill cry of a hunter rang through
The silence and echoed through the *polje*
And over the grey, limestone houses of Prvo Selo,
And two birds of prey, hawks of some sort,
Glided into my periphery like bomber planes,
Flying low over the nearby borderline
Between the closest fields of the *polje*
And the edge of the village.
Father scrambled for the binoculars,
But I stayed and watched the two of them
Glide low, elegantly and in single file,
Up in the lowest gusty thermals.
Then they were gone.
No definitive identification.
There, at the porch table, I obsessed
Excitedly about *birds of prey*.

And suddenly, a praying mantis.
On the stone wall, to my right.
Grass-green on the grey of the stone wall,
Small and serene, in a utopia of insectile peace.
In meditation on the wall,
Like a Buddhist monk facing the vast cosmos of sacred nothingness.
Small on the wall, vulnerable, like a child in the world.
A melancholy beauty about her, clinging to the house
In her green and peaceful insectitude,
Like a nostalgic in a place of memories,
In deep quiet remembrance, with a sombre smile.

The soft stillness of the *polje*
Beneath the cool, sea-blue sky.


Note: *polje*, valley (Croatian)

Chris Agee

I'd forgotten that half-an-hour-or-so
until a few days before our bus swung in again
to the sloping roadside restaurant
perched on an overlook high above
the dazzling Neretva threaded below
the white conical minarets and strip fields, the Yugoslav pylons

of beautiful Jablanica. A pumped and cobblestoned rill
was bubbling from top to bottom, through a series
of gutters, waterwheels, pipes and cement fish-tanks
where trout were penned in dappled beauty.
Eight lamb-spits filled the air with woodsmoke and its smell.
I remember a quick lunch and nothing of Miriam

but love and presence. At the back, in the woods
below the dining deck, a breath of presence,
ash-flicker and mapleleaf flutter
in the high heat of Central Europe.
I stood perspirant with Jacob and watched far below
a brown, pebbled, submarine sandbar

like a trout's speckled belly
in the crook of a wooded bend –
depths turquoise, shallows green,
under another day's
dazzling
blue river.

Marianne Burton

THE PERSISTENCE OF VISION

It is as if our eyelids had been cut off.
Light reflecting from the whitewashed church
outside the hotel room, sears our retinas.

Each Easter day dawns hot as August,
lemons bleaching to ripeness as we watch.
Blossom dies in the orchards, buds wilt,

boutiques are cleared of summer stock.
We clap tight our shutters to shake out
shorts and gaudy T-shirts in the shade.

Each late morning we saunter to the beach
in swimsuits, while mass celebrants
pass us like crows, shrouded in mantillas.

Each late evening we cruise to restaurants,
while bells ring and silent hooded lines
process religious statues through the streets.

This last afternoon the light is so intense
I want to set it down as memory, to sketch
you curled on the bed, naked as a faun,

as St Sebastian. The bells toll deeper.
I varnish my nails until they flutter in
a blood-red rosary. The light still shines

and when I shut my eyes, the window brace
burns behind my lids in the shape of a cross
for a long moment. Before it fades away.

Kenneth Steven

THE GHOST ORCHID

One day, when the air is sore to breathe
And the seas are dead and heavy, thudding
Over empty shores, and only a dwindling of us

Remain – strange, in hiding,
From yellow and red skies,
From scabbed earth –

We will draw in caves
The eerie shapes
Of everything we remember;

We will weave out of firelight
What fields meant, what horses were,
The story of flowing water, of birds bringing morning into song.

And for a while
Before we have grown old
Like moss on rocks, furred and searching with age,

Our children will believe
It was that beautiful,
That good.

Eamon Cooke

NORTHWEST

Low moan. A winter wind.
Bitter and cold

The darkening day.
A gull crosses the sky

Searching for food.
A soul searches for faith.

Encroaching on all sides
The dim borders of despair.

\*


In spring
A car drives northwest
Passing fields, trees
Hedgerows, random homes.

Takes, near Roosky
The dual carriageway.

(Bright cumulus clouds
Above the horizon).

Diverts, before Carrick
For Jamestown cemetery.

A family grave is visited.
Near-hand the Shannon

Murmurs like a prayer
Breathes

A known music.
Faith and hope are restored.

Brian Turner

THE EUPHRATES WHEEL

Tell me a secret: whisper history into my ear,
not of emirs and palaces lacquered in gold,
not of nations and politics and conquest;
speak to me of love and loss, what it is
to be human, and alive, what makes us
pull a trigger or kiss one another;
whisper of the coffins and of the men hung
dark over the Euphrates, of women crying,
of a man and woman walking slow one dawn
with a shovel and a blanket, gone
to bury their dead child in the orange groves;
tell me the sound of a child's laughter
is water in the wheel, a blue song
when it falls, some of what war can bring,
more than one should ever bear, and tell me
all that might sustain us.

## INTERVIEW WITH PADDY BUSHE

Born Dublin 1948. Both parents from a rural background. Father worked
in Valuation Office, so, as part of his work schedule, the family was able to
spend long summer holidays on the west coast, mainly Kerry. Educated
Marino CBS (primary), Coláiste Mhuire CBS (secondary), UCD (BA
English, Irish, 1969, H. Dip. In Ed. 1970). Married Fíona 1970 and spent
1971-73 in Australia. Began teaching in Waterville, Kerry in 1973. Two
children, Ciairín and Éanna. Had begun writing in teens and at college.
Published poems mainly in Irish. From about 1969 to early 1980s, did not
write at all, and had stopped seeing himself as a writer. Attended workshops
in Listowel during 1980s. First collection, *Poems With Amergin* (Beaver Row)
published 1989. Retired from teaching 1990. Living and working in
Waterville. Began to travel again at the dawn of the twenty-first century.

PIR: *Your early poems were written in Irish, but your first collection,* Poems
with Amergin, *appeared in English. Can you say why you switched from Irish
at that time?*

PB: I had always written some poems in English, but, yes, almost all of
my early poems were in Irish. I suppose that was an ideological decision,
a literary side-effect of the 'constitutional imperative' which I now believe
did a great disservice to the Irish language. In a variation of 'in the
country of the blind, the one-eyed man is king', I think that, nationally,
we tried to close one eye – whether that was the Gaelic eye or the Anglo-
Irish eye – rather than to embrace the bilingual richness that our history
offered us. This gave us the wonderful poetry of Michael Hartnett's *A
Farewell to English*, or Seán Ó Ríordáin's 'Fill Arís', but it was very
limiting. Even more limiting was the post-colonial, usually monolingual
dismissal of Irish. I see-sawed across this linguistic/ideological divide for
many years, in a very blinkered way. It was a shaky basis on which to
choose a writing language. But now – and I hope I'm not deceiving myself
– I tend to write in whichever language a particular poem, or group of
poems, seems most at home in. This may be an over-simplification, but
there are aspects of myself and my imaginative concerns that make
themselves known to me in Irish, others in English, and I hope my work
reflects this.

*You say that from about 1969, when you were about 21, you stopped writing,
and could not see yourself as a writer? Why was that? And was it the workshops
in Listowel, presumably during Writers' Week, that got you going again?*

I am still not sure why I stopped. I suppose I could say I was timid, and lacked confidence; but that was still true when I started to write again, and remains true to this day. Like many other writers, I would say, I am often amazed at my temerity in publishing a poem or a collection. I suppose teaching, setting up home, family, all these contributed to my seeing myself as being other than a writer. But, again with hindsight, perhaps I was serving a kind of apprenticeship, grounding myself in a way I had not been as a child. I grew up in suburban Dublin, which had no imaginative hold over me; nor, indeed, did the city itself. Maybe I needed the rooting which living in the Iveragh peninsula gave me, in order to let my imagination blossom from a soil which was both real and imaginatively alive to me.

And yes, Listowel Writers' Week and its workshops allowed me to see myself as a writer again. Brendan Kennelly, Michael Hartnett, yourself and others, the companionship of other tentative aspirants, the whole participatory atmosphere in what was then, back in the 1980s, a far less star-studded festival, all of this was hugely stimulating. I had written a poem called 'After Love' which, believe it or not, had come to me in a dream. I brought it to Listowel, was encouraged, and I have been writing, with increasing seriousness, ever since.

*Your recent long poem in* Poetry Ireland Review *(issue 110), 'Suite on the Suppression of the Performing Arts in Tech Amergin', comments fairly, and in strong terms, on the failure of certain bodies to value the arts: do you see a future for Tech Amergin in Waterville, and indeed for those who are trying to promote the arts in areas outside the large cities? Feel free to comment further on the failure in Waterville's case.*

Tech Amergin, in its primary role as an adult education centre, would as of now seem to be secure. This is a function which its managing body, KES (Kerry Education Service, formerly Co Kerry VEC) is familiar with. However, its role as an arts centre, which was developed exclusively on a local voluntary basis, and which resulted in a one million euro theatre / gallery development, funded entirely by the Department of Arts as a result of that exclusively local and voluntary initiative, seem to be beyond the capacity or interest of KES. That lack of commitment meant that for a few years KES simply took no interest in the arts programme which a voluntary management group organised, with the help of local authority funding and in cooperation with the centre manager and staff, a programme widely recognised as being of astonishing range and quality. No member of KES management ever attended even one play, classical concert or traditional session. We found this puzzling, even disappointing, but it seemed at the time to be a benign indifference. We should have realised that the apparent indifference masked an underlying hostility. Perhaps KES resented the success of the voluntary group in achieving something which its own inertia would not allow it even to imagine. In any case, when the voluntary management group successfully resisted a KES attempt to reduce by 50% the hours of the centre manager, a move which would have had disastrous implications for the educational programme there, the bureaucracy took umbrage. KES took its institutional revenge by getting rid of the voluntary group which had developed the centre. Its weapon – and its target – was the arts programme. Through a process of deceit and intimidation, it took control of the arts funding, forcing the cancellation of the arts programme and the collective resignation of the voluntary group which had secured both the million-euro funding for the centre itself and the local authority funding for the arts programme. Due to a KES contractual decision, it is not the centre manager's job to run an arts programme. In the 18 months since the forced resignation of the voluntary management group, there has been almost no arts programme; what there has been has happened only in response to public statements and media reports about the misuse of arts funding. And the minimal programme there has been over the summer does not involve the subsidisation for which the local authority funding is intended. Effectively, public arts funding has been appropriated from the arts by KES, and the people of the remote Iveragh peninsula have been robbed of an arts programme which Arts Minister Jimmy Deenihan had described as being a model for other rural areas. The Minister initially described the KES action as 'crazy', and subsequently raised the possibility of KES being asked to repay the Department of Arts' one million investment. He then, however, found himself either unwilling or unable to take on the institutional vested interests involved, which operated within and between the bureaucracies of KES, its sister organisation Kerry Co Council and, indeed, a middle-rank official in the Minister's own department, who acted in such a way as to undermine the Minister's initial support for the voluntary group as well as the reputation of the chairperson of that group.

That Kerry Co Council would be complicit in allowing local authority arts funding to be subsumed into another local authority body, without being spent on the arts, is deeply depressing, but it will probably come as no surprise to those in the arts community who are familiar with the reputation of that body as having probably the worst record of any local authority in its support for the arts. Incidentally the former Arts Minister John O'Donoghue, during whose time as Minister the million euro investment was made, has publicly stated that the arts in Iveragh are being neglected and that 'KES is the problem'.

Theo Dorgan, having chaired a public seminar at which an audience of over 200 people gave their unanimous support to the voluntary group, wrote a detailed and valuable report on that seminar and recommendations therefrom. I circulated this report, in which Theo went out of his way to be balanced, to the official bodies involved. None of them responded. This was insulting not only to Theo, but to the public which had left the Minister and the Cathaoirleach of KES in no doubt about its dissatisfaction with that body's role in the suppression of the arts programme which had been run by the voluntary group. Incidentally, at this seminar, the Cathaoirleach of KES appears to have deliberately misled the audience when, in response to a direct question, he indicated that KES was willing to enter into a mediation process suggested by the Minister. This turned out to be untrue, something which was no surprise to us, but which raises very serious questions of integrity in the dealings of a public body with the public.

Am I hopeful? The last two years have been deeply depressing and disillusioning. Institutional bullying is more insidious than individual bullying, because the bullies can hide behind the resources and anonymity of their institution. That a bureaucracy would feel antagonistic towards a group or an individual is understandable; but I was shocked that organisations and individuals with a public service role would allow that antagonism to take precedence over the interests of the public they nominally serve. The members of the voluntary group have their own rich cultural lives. It is an already disadvantaged and marginalised population, rather than the volunteers, which really suffers the effects of what one very senior political figure, who is familiar with the situation, told me was 'the worst form of bureaucratic bullying'. I believe that what has happened is a public financial scandal and a social tragedy. But if all official bodies, and their political heads, were to have a genuine commitment to providing an arts programme of the same range and quality as that which the voluntary group ran for many years, the situation could be easily resolved. For rural areas, where an interested voluntary group is willing to develop the arts, state or local authority bodies need only have a benevolent interest for the arts to thrive. Minimal funding will suffice. However, where the bureaucratic interest is arrogant, mendacious or even malevolent, as it came to be in Waterville, then those bureaucratic hands will choke the arts, and spend taxpayers' money doing so.

I have to believe that decency, goodwill and genuine public service will prevail in the end, even though there is little evidence of that at this time. On the positive side, I have to say that my experience of having to deal with the rather serpentine thought processes of a bureaucracy whose nest has been disturbed has opened me up to a type of public poetry which I had generally resisted. It's probably a good thing to lie down in the snake-pit for a while!

*Your poetry insists on imaginative probing of one's territory; in 'To Make the Stone Sing' your wrote of Cill Rialaig, an early Christian monastic site where 'the monks once peeled / the world from their lives / and shed their selves / in search of another'. You have travelled a great deal, to Nepal, for instance, visiting the past, remote and difficult places. This feels like pilgrimage to me. Of the monks you also wrote: 'I deny, envy, and fear their illumination.' Can you comment on the notion of pilgrimage in your work and take that word 'fear' a little further?*

I hasten to say that I am not some intrepid explorer. I have been lucky enough, in the last fifteen years or so, to visit some strange and wonderful places with my wife Fíona. But I am what I think of as a 'Lonely Planeteer', one of an extraordinarily lucky generation who can pretend we're young, buy rucksacks and get to walk in the Himalaya, or Greenland or western China, or wherever. Before that, I suppose, I did a great deal of exploring in my adoptive territory of Iveragh, much of which centred on old routes and sites of pilgrimage. There was Skellig Michael, that bare exposed rocky island of such extraordinary physical beauty and spiritual resonance; Drung Hill, a major Lughnasa site and territorial boundary at many levels; Inis Uasal, or Church Island, a monastic island full of sibilant echoes. Imaginatively, also, the whole Milesian myth, especially the Amergin poem, became enormously important to me, after I discovered that my house overlooked his landing place, the shoreline where he declaimed his famous appropriation of Ireland. So yes, imaginative probing of territory has been, and remains, central to my poetry, even when I'm writing about politics, love or other things with no obvious connection to any particular territory.

In relation to my poetry, I'm not sure if 'pilgrimage' is the right word, except perhaps in a residual and certainly very secular way. I emphatically do not believe in God, gods or an afterlife. I emphatically do believe, on the other hand, in the importance of an imaginative, ethical and philosophical engagement with otherness, whether that otherness is cultural, chronological, spatial, historical, geographical, aesthetic, socio-political or whatever. This is what spirituality means to me, and I believe that if we lose this sort of engagement, and engage with our world on an exclusively rational or materialistic basis, we lose what is precious in our humanity. So I suppose my poetry, and the experiences which gave rise to it, is a pilgrimage in this sense. And, for me, a part of this engagement is what Coleridge called a 'willing suspension of disbelief'. I do not abandon disbelief, but I think it is good to suspend it so that we can enter into the mind and soul of others, and be illuminated by what they may literally believe, or have believed. This is how we engage with literature; I think the same sort of engagement with other aspects of life can be enormously enriching, and can enhance our own lives and the lives of others. And of course I was brought up as a believer, was a committed and entranced altar-boy, in love with Latin ritual and the headiness of incense, considered entering the priesthood, and, until I was in my very late teens, in no doubt as to the existence of God, afterlife, judgement, divine law and all the other absolutes that made life straightforward, if not easy. It was many years before the judgemental, eschatological side of my religious upbringing loosened its grip. I am glad that it has done so, while remaining grateful for much of its moral insight. I doubt if the aesthetic, imaginative aspect of the whole thing will ever loosen its grip. Nor, I think, would I wish it to do so. Which is all a roundabout way of saying why I 'envy their illumination'. I think I 'feared' their illumination primarily because when I wrote that poem, about twenty years ago, belief at some level still had me by the eschatological throat, and I feared both the consequences of being wrong and the empty purposelessness that being right opened up before me. I no longer have that fear in either sense, and I don't think I would write that line today.

*Your poetic forms are rooted in the quatrain; if you are seeking some form of surety, or security in life, do you find a source of this in using that form?*

Even though I have sometimes been described as a formalist, the use of a particular form is not usually important for me, and very rarely premeditated. In general, I try to let a poem fall into its own shape without pushing it. Sometimes a poem will end up in quite a free shape, sometimes it will be as formal as a villanelle. I've even written villanelles in Irish.

I honestly don't know the answer to your question. I suppose I am trying to find shape and security in my life and in my writing, so perhaps using the quatrain, as you suggest, is reflective of this. I don't know this for sure, but I suspect it may come from the great love I have for traditional songs such as 'Dónal Óg' or 'Úr-Chill a' Chreagáin', which are written in quatrains or octets. I would love to be able to compose such intensely luminous lyrics. Since my schooldays, I have loved how Coleridge achieved the same luminosity and intensity in 'The Rime of the Ancient Mariner', and the cadences of Richard Burton's wonderful recording of that poem are a constant presence. So, am I looking for intensity in predictable and controlled measures? Probably.

*How important is the 'other', the remote, to your imagination; you know Donne's phrase, to make 'one little room an everywhere'. The collection* The Nitpicking of Cranes *in particular moves very far afield, and returns. You touch on the remote as almost 'insubstantial' to your senses, but return with the mud of such places 'clinging to my boots'. It reads as if you (Everyman) order the photographs of such places 'in the drawer / Of my imagination' and yet everywhere you carry 'the blackness within'. A pilgrimage is always towards something; but it may also be away from something?*

That line of Donne's was in fact the basis for the first poem of that collection, 'John Donne in Beijing', which was really a love poem which tried to draw the exotic, the homely and the literary into a loose sonnet. *The Nitpicking of Cranes*, as you say, moved far afield. But it was important to me that, as you equally note, that it should return. And it was important that that return should happen while I was far afield, that I should be on home ground while I was away. That is probably why a number of poems in Irish insisted on their place in the collection, and why, for example, a poem set in a small ethnic museum in Yunnan in south-western China became a commentary on the disproportionate influence of the dead on contemporary Ireland. Remoteness, otherness, the insubstantial – yes, these are fundamental to me. But they become remote, other or insubstantial only in relation to the concrete, the here and now. You cannot have 'the other' without 'this and that'.

I do unfortunately carry a 'blackness within'; it is sometimes fairly overwhelming. For many years I tried to escape from it in alcohol, with disastrous results. Intense engagement with poetry certainly can alleviate it, but sometimes I cannot engage with poetry because of it. Perhaps I am on a permanent pilgrimage away from this darkness. Love, family – with both of which I have been blessedly lucky – are also great healers, the primary ones, in fact.

*Your most unified collection, perhaps also the most structured, is the latest,* My Lord Buddha of Carraig Éanna: *here you bounce the sacred off the secular, the eternal off the temporal, in a wide depth and range of reference, chiming again off the central focus of your work, the Skelligs. The placing of the statue of Buddha on the edge of a cliff behind your house was a deliberate act: it faces the Skelligs, it speaks of settled contentment with the difficult. The poems in this collection also range across themes of love and companionship. In all of this, can you speak of the balance you are working towards, what Thomas Kinsella might call 'order', in the ostensibly unbalanced and disordered world of our time?*

I'm not sure that it's the most unified, but it is certainly the most settled, the most contented – 'Equanimity, now and again. Equilibrium' – as the first line of the title poem says. In simple terms, it is my happiest book, which is no small thing, and I am grateful for that. If I had been told twenty years ago that I would be writing a fortieth wedding anniversary poem about walking the Annapurna Circuit, in all its literally breathless wonder and its aching highs and lows of body and spirit, I would have laughed, enviously but dismissively. But there we were, and here is the poem and I am filled with gratitude.

Rather than thinking of it as the sacred bouncing of the secular, or the temporal off the eternal, I prefer to think of the secular being the sacred, the temporal being the eternal. And, crucially, I think of the exotic being the commonplace and vice versa. I tried to say this in the title and even in the cover photograph.

Am I working towards balance and order? I honestly don't know. I feel I stumble across things rather than work towards them. And when I do construct a pattern of balance and order, I am constantly reminded that it is a construct, an ordering of the world that is artificial. But this artificial construction, what Wallace Stevens called the Supreme Fiction, is necessary for us to function as morally and ethically sensitive social beings. This is why, to my mind, we invented God: a Darwinian survival mechanism which allows us to live with comfort, dignity and moments of joy which have no objective basis.

### Other Collections
*Digging Towards The Light* (Dedalus Press, 1994)
*To Make The Stone Sing* (Sceilg Press / Wolfhound Press, 1996)
*In Ainneoin na gCloch* (Coiscéim, 2001)
*Hopkins on Skellig Michael* (Dedalus Press, 2001)
*The Nitpicking Of Cranes* (Dedalus Press, 2004)
*Gile na Gile* (Coiscéim, 2005)
*To Ring In Silence: New and Selected Poems* (Dedalus Press, 2009)
*My Lord Buddha of Carraig Éanna* (Dedalus Press, 2012)

### Translation
*Teanga* (Coiscéim, 1991), into Irish from the Scottish Gaelic of Iain
    Mac a' Ghobhainn (Ian Crichton Smith)
*The Ghost Man / An Góstfhear* (Coiscéim, 2004), into English from the
    Chinese of Zhang Ye, with versions in Irish by Gabriel Rosenstock
*Rogha Dánta / Selected Poems* (Cló Iar-Chonnachta, 2005), from the Irish
    of Gabriel Rosenstock
*Ó Choill go Barr Ghéaráin* (Coiscéim, 2013), the collected poems of
    Somhairle Mac Gill-Eain / Sorley MacLean

### As Editor
*Duanaire Mhaidhcí* (Coiscém, 2006)
*Voices at the World's Edge: Irish Poets on Skellig Michael* (Dedalus Press, 2010)

Martina Evans

DADDY AND MAE WEST
  – *for my brother Richard Cotter, in memory of our father,
    Richard Cotter 1902-1988*

*Come up and see me some time,* you said, patting the yellow Formica
with swollen crooked hands, the morning Mae died and Mammy said
there was more to you than met the eye, half laughing and half
annoyed too, as if Mae might have some claim on you. You were old
enough to be my grandfather and that wasn't always easy when you
were referred to as such and the truth is you didn't believe in washing
much maybe you were saving water for you were as pathologically
tight as a concentration camp survivor, knotted laces, rusty nails, *Old
Moore's Almanacs*, the salvage fashion was waiting for you. Every now
and then there was a clean sweep and scrub and you were bereft as I
am now, reading my brother's email about the farm in the Forties.
You did sing but rarely to an audience, I remember *Fill Up Once More*
and *Glorio, Glorio, to the bold Fenian Men* but I was a child caught up in
days of wishing, why wouldn't you wash? My brother says that your
favourite was *Felons of Our Land* and he heard you sing *The Four Leaf
Shamrock* at Yellowtown, your tenor playing against a thick rapt
silence. You'd gone there to have a farm implement fixed. That word.
I hear you now frustrated in the Seventies, asking had any of us seen
your *implement*. You used old expressions like *By Jove* and called bowls
*vessels*. But my brother saw you dancing – you. *Traditional ballroom
dancing* my brother writes and *he did the Russian Sailor dance, kicking
his legs while down on his haunches.* Come up and see me some time, I
want to say. Come dancing.

## Martina Evans

THROUGH THE LOOKING GLASS
 – *for Helen Lynch*

Auntie Helen had a shop too
and even though it was also Spar
it smelt sweeter than ours
the wood-effect lino softer
like toffee under my tan sandals
and when she brought us out of
her diminutive sitting room –
where I sat looking at
the yellow teapot in the shape
of a house – the fluorescent strip
of light fluttered and sang.
Mars and Milky Way
tasted different here – they
were forbidden and had to be
stolen at home. Here I sat
quietly spending in my mind
my first wage packet when
I would buy a teapot in the shape of
a house, listening
to the flat-to-the-floor Limerick accents.
Auntie Helen was funnier than
Mammy, told the sharpest stories
with her sad brown-eyed face.
At the end, the sisters
always cried, and we said goodbye
their imploding faces mirrored
in the black night in the shop window,
with its red-lettered statement
*it's cheaper by far to shop at Spar*
and it always seemed to be rain
on the road to Charleville
with the white paper bag of sweets
open on my lap.

## Geraldine Mitchell

BASSO CONTINUO
 – *for Vedran Smailović*

It begins with a summer concert, wine. Red wine
carmine on white linen, evening light. Schubert's
Quintet in C. One cellist knows the score by heart,
turns his head, sees concentric rings

pulse in every glass. That night he dreams: a field,
bright air, the absent smell of death. No flies,
no sign the earth has been disturbed. He knows,
yet does not know he knows, what lies below or why.

No movement but his bow, his elbow back and forth.
Hoarse words hauled up, grim adagio.
He sows a solemn beauty and moves on:
another field, another town, another country.

Around our only world and round again, concentric
rings lapping the shores of every human heart.

Winner in the Published Poet Category of the Poetry Ireland /
Trócaire Poetry Competition 2012

## Allison McVety

COATTAILS

> *Girl falls from a roof looking for comet,* New York Times
> *(Amy Hopkins, 19 May 1910)*

When I fall, I fall big-time and not for the boys either.
It's for you. You who've kept your promise
across the centuries tonight come close enough
for me to grab your coattails and fly.
Leave the charlatans to their cure-pills,
leave the papers to their harbingers and doomsdays.
How can I, at a time like this, be anything
if not alive? I think starlight must taste like snow.
The universe leans in as we pass where you
have been: a beam of gas and dust, a trail
of far-off news and magic. So when I fall,
when I actually fall, I'm looking at you.
The glass roof of the airshaft shatters in welcome.
I have a glittering tail; I am a gift for Brooklyn.

# Liam Carson

## THE JOURNEY IN AND THE JOURNEY OUT

Liam Ó Muirthile, *An Fuíoll Feá – Rogha Dánta / Woodcuttings – New and Selected Poems* (Cois Life, 2013), hb with CD, €30.

> I'm a native English speaker; I come from the city centre of Cork. I'm a city boy, I played hurling in the streets. I grew up with the mods and rockers and corner boys, steering-cars, the smell of the river Lee. A lot of my psyche is English language. You could say that the acquisition of Irish is a forgery – you're forging a consciousness, you're layering this stuff with the Irish language.

So spoke poet Liam Ó Muirthile in an interview with *Fortnight* magazine. It would be a mistake to read 'forgery' as 'fake' or 'bogus'. In Ó Muirthile's author's note to *An Fuíoll Feá – Rogha Dánta / Woodcuttings – New and Selected Poems*, he speaks of how 'an integrated language must emanate from the unconscious'. The 'conscious' and 'unconscious' are words that pepper Ó Muirthile's view of poetry. 'We have to reach an authentic voice. You just can't fake it. My journeying into language is journeying into the unconscious. That's the only thing that's important – to render the unconscious conscious'.

Ó Muirthile's poetic project is nothing less than a journey in and out of language ('an turas isteach agus an turas amach'). That journey has much to do with his upbringing in Cork City, and an awareness of Irish language structures and thought-patterns pulsing beneath English – 'or more properly Anglo-Irish, which is both an unnerving and exciting sensual and aural experience'.

Of Cork he has written: 'It was possible, even in the late Sixties, to imagine an authentic Irish language voice of the English-speaking city. Nowhere else in Ireland had the written text of the language been worked so late into the nineteenth century by dairy farmers, tradesmen, tailors, stonecutters, teachers, Catholic and some Protestant clergy, and professional scribes with commitment and playfulness, and with an enduring sense of regional and local identity.'

*An Fuíoll Feá* is, by any standard, a remarkable book. It is a selected collection, but weighs in at over 500 pages. It is, somewhat astonishingly, Ó Muirthile's first bi-lingual collection, and is a long overdue project. The translations are mostly by Gabriel Rosenstock, whose fine versions retain the tone of the originals, charged with an airy clarity. Other translators include Dermot Bolger, Ciaran Carson, Greg Delanty, Paul Muldoon and Peter Sirr.

It is also a brilliantly constructed collection, and it is worth reading the poems in the order in which they are presented. One poem will often flow seamlessly into the next, the poems cross-reference and riff off each other. In the collection's opening poem, 'Fúm fhéin' (the title is translated by Gabriel Rosenstock as 'Freewheeling', a conscious reference to Bob Dylan), Ó Muirthile sets out his stall: 'agus mé ag lorg slí isteach / i ndán ar an mboth' ('as I seek a way in / to a poem in the hut'). The hut appears again in 'Gréagaigh' ('Greeks') – 'Mhaireadar sna botháin / tar éis a gcuid eachtraí farraige' (Shacked up in huts / their sea sagas over').

Many of Ó Muirthile's poems respond to and reference music. 'Bóithre Nár Ceadaíodh' ('Unexplored Roads') describes a journey through the back roads of Forkhill in search of the grave of poet Peadar Ó Doirnín. Ó Muirthile describes himself 'Ag breith chugam féin, / ag lorg múnla nua, éalú fiú' ('Getting to grips with myself, / looking for a new model, escaping even'). Within music he seeks the trigger for a new form of expression, allowing him 'to view some shape previously unseen':

> meascán *folk-rock*, sean-nóis,
> *blues* a chaitheamh isteach
> sa bhrú-bhruthaire féachaint
> cén cruth nár fíoraíodh cheana

'Idir Dhá Fhonn Mhalla' ('Between Two Slow Airs') reprises themes of journeying, language and music. As Ó Muirthile and a friend drive through Cavan, 'looking for the word mud / in a placename, / one that had lodged in the back of my mind' ('ag faire amach / don bhfocal pluda i logainm amháin, / ceann a d'fhan i gcúl an chinn'), they find it has eluded them. Here language is 'as a shadow that passes through the soul':

> mar a ghabhann scáil tríd an anam
> is a lonnaíonn go buan ann ina anamscáil

There's often a potent physicality to Ó Muirthile's poems. In 'Port an Phíobaire' ('The Piper's Tune', translated by Ciaran Carson), he envisions the uillean pipes as a 'béist', a fierce animal-like contraption, that breathes, snorts and gulders. There's a tremendous energy to its final verse:

> le stail na filíochta ag léimt thar clathacha,
> is port an phíobaire ag imeacht cosa in airde
> le marcshlua na uillíochta

> or like a stallion of poetry jumping ditches,
> the piper's tune galloping hell for leather
> like the Universal Cavalry

What is remarkable about Ó Muirthile is the sheer breadth and depth of both themes and forms in his work. There are short lyrics celebrating bardic poets Ó Bruadair, Ó Rathaille and Eoghan Rua Ó Súilleabháin. There are poems that deal with craft – woodcutting, sculpture, etching; poems of the sea, shipwrecks, the Blasket Islands, and herons; poems paying homage to Rory Gallagher and Michael Hartnett; and poems about hurling. There are two short blackbird poems that echo the ninth century 'The Blackbird at Belfast Lough'. Long narrative poems such as 'Banaltra' ('Nurse') and 'Walking Time' remind one of the sprawling lines and dramatic drive of C K Williams – and are also tender evocations of familial love. There are gorgeous poems that sing of simple pleasures, of a zen-like awareness of 'searmanas saolta an lae' ('the worldly ceremony of the day').

Ó Muirthile is also fond of the prose poem – 'Meáchan Rudaí' ('The Weight of Things') is a tour-de-force litany in which the word 'meáchan' is repeated again and again, with increasing weight and force, creating a deeply moving portrait of his mother. One wishes that his response to the Omagh bombing, 'Cnoc an Áir', had been included here. It is a harrowing chant of grief, of which he had the following to say: 'I was standing at Hill 16 in Croke Park watching Waterford and Kilkenny playing. But what can you do? You have to find that grief within yourself and within the language. I'd see that as a form of public poetry. It was the function of the poet within the Irish language to be public griever. "Cnoc an Áir" ('the hill of slaughter') had the ring of the Fiannaíocht. Language does contain something inherent in the sounds.'

And it is sound which draws Ó Muirthile to Irish. Of the poem 'ÁÍÉÓÚ', Ó Muirthile has said: 'I had to get back to that point – ÁÉÍÓÚ – learning the sounds of the language, to find out what was there, what was hidden behind those sounds. That took me back to bardic poetry. The bardic poems have an energy within them, it's like an egg that hasn't been warmed yet. There's a wholeness in them, it's almost a hermetically sealed world. They contain *themselves*, like sound-boxes. Once I resolved ÁÉÍÓÚ for myself, it freed up a lot of stuff. I became conscious of *language* in a new way'.

In his essay 'Offshore on Land' (published in *A New View of the Irish Language*, Cois Life, 2008), Ó Muirthile made the pessimistic statement that 'the poem in Irish is in freefall. Literacy in the language has all but collapsed … since 1968.' On one level he's dead right, and the blindness of many Irish writers and readers to what is happening in Irish-language poetry is cause for concern. This is echoed in the opening dark notes of 'Sanas' ('Gloss'): 'Focail óir / iompaithe ina luaidhe / le casadh an leathanaigh' ('Golden words / become ashes / at the turning of a page'). It is to his credit, though, that he goes beyond this pessimism in search of

'Ailceimic úrnua' ('Brand new alchemy'), positing 'mo theanga' ('my language') as 'Béarla-Gaeilge'. Here there's a hint of Seán Ó Riordáin's 'an teanga seo leath-liom' ('this language half-mine'), albeit reversed, and with the stigma excised.

Hence we find Ó Muirthile breaking free of the weight of linguistic responsibility, and he has often stated his distaste for 'language puritanism'. If the Cork English of his childhood had Irish bubbling under its surface, poems such as 'Fast Dán' ('Fast Poem') and 'Speed Dán' ('Speed Poem') play with the notion of English bubbling under Irish. There's a joyful lightness at work here that eschews 'ualach cré teanga' ('a load of linguistic earth'), urging poetry to shoot up 'ina fhás aon lae' – 'like an unabashed mushroom'.

'Sanas', it might be noted, contains more meanings than 'gloss' alone might imply, and is defined in Dineen's dictionary as 'special knowledge, occult knowledge, a secret, a suggestion, a hint … a farewell, a greeting'. It's also a palindrome, with a hint of constant return, of a linguistic journey that has no beginning and no end. Or as Ó Muirthile himself put it: 'It's to go down as many cul-de-sacs, as many boreens, as many diversions as you can manage, and come back again. It's also – to use a much-abused word – a spiritual journey. It's a life-long attention, a task.'

It cannot be stated firmly enough that *An Fuíoll Feá* is one of the most important poetry collections to be published in Ireland for some time. It's a finely produced book, and comes with a CD of Ó Muirthile and Rosenstock reading the poems. Ó Muirthile's work is superbly crafted, and within that craft burns the flame of true poetry.

Or as 'Speed Dán' puts it:

> le lastóir *zip* trí thine
> ó bhos go bos sa tsráid,
> ró-the le breith air, ró-the
> ar fad don teagmháil

> as a flaming fire-lighter
> tossing it from one hand to the other,
> too hot to handle, too much
> to touch

# Philip Coleman

A YEAR LATER

*14 January 2013*

Just in the door
    not even
when the call came
    of your passing –

dear Pearse
    with Bach playing
sunlight facing
    that afternoon.

You told me
    how often
keep trying
    *why not?*

A hidden radio
    in a drawer ...
*Scenes of Clerical Life,*
    Wallace Stevens –

Geneva, Leeds,
    Barcelona,
Dublin – a voice
    singing, remembering.

Always making
    your words
present perfect
    alight illumine.

# Billy Ramsell

HENRIETTA STREET
  i.m. *John Kelly RHA*

You must know, sitting up in the lilac machine-light,
in the midnight stillness of intensive care,
as a machine does most of your breathing for you
and you sketch your own face over and over
on half-inch thick New Somerset paper
('two pounds a sheet', you'd quipped to the orderly,
'and when I'm finished each page is worth nothing').

You prick lead and smudge it
into the fibres,
in that medical silence interrupted

by next door's coughing like brown paper crackling,
a lilting giggle from the nurses' station
and the hushing rush of the C-PAP machine;

that winking, beeping desk beside your pillow,
with its length of see-through tubing you think of as the coil,
with its nozzle strapped over your half-willing mouth.

It pushes air down through the branching trachea,
diminishes the V/Q mismatch,
and holds the alveoli open
that if closed will never expand again.

It lets oxygen roam through the corridors,
then through the tiny, tangled shafts of circulation,
to your eyelids, your irises,
your fingers splayed on the creamy sheet's surface,
to your clasping index and thumb
that unclasp the 6B you've been clasping

when you see
not your eyes which you'd just pencilled in
but Icarus's careful eyes looking back at you

and you knuckle your forehead,
like the keyless at the moment when the door slams shut,

as it comes to you not for the first time,
but more suddenly, unutterably now in the hospital,
that in painting your life for so long you'd never quite witnessed it.

You'd told me that.
In The Clock or The Welcome Inn I think it was
or some boozer on the northside grown beyond designation,
its name rotted like the carpet and the locks in the jacks.
I remember a pewter-coloured Tuesday
in the guilty lull before rush-hour, when beer's yeasty zest
had loosened me enough to broach such things. You said:

It's all just ashes, Billy, all the pictures I made are just ashes.
What do the images come to, all those tinctures and shapes,
weighed next to the thousand sensations
of walking for milk to the corner?
I relished the scents of acid and turpentine, the thick smell of paint,
when I should have been out sniffing lilacs or what have you.
I spent year after year staring into that mirror, that subtle mirror,
when I should have been looking out the window at the world.

Those hazel, light-devouring eyes
from when you painted him over and over,
Icarus Puppet, Icarus Resting, Icarus Astray,
till they cluttered your fourth-storey studio,

till you'd made a race of watchers
looking out from diluted tangerine backgrounds,
from their backgrounds of vermillion,
their vast lop-sided heads quizzical, indifferent,
but their wings for the most part furled,
shy of imposing their feathered hybridity,

till the day came when you fled from their gazes
down all the rickety stairs to Henrietta Street:

a terrace of palaces
in flaking red brick

that in the accumulating February dusk
stressed its shabby grandeur,
its nobility and dereliction.

And on the breeze there was a tang of rain,
the breeze inundating that trench
of moist and shadowy Georgiana

in freshets that carried you past
the boarded-up ground storey flats,
   two fat barristers
     wobbling
   over the cobbles,
and the open side-door of the King's Inn pub
       (the row of gleaming optics,
         the curdling, sun-starved skin of a regular
         in the poker-machine dimness),
then through a blue, papillionic billow of schoolgirls
released from St Carmel's,
   their skirts hitched up inches past regulation.

The wind swirled their gossip, their washed electric scent after you.

And as you stepped into Moore Street
you knew something had happened

for the fruit-sellers stood there open-mouthed
and the fish-wives were stalled in their banter

and all the cheerful butchers of Moore Street,
and all their apprentices,
muttered and argued in their doorways
in huddled incredulity at what they'd seen:

the boy with bird's wings they'd watched gobsmacked,
unmoving to a man,
their angled, gaping faces tracking the creature
as he grew from point to miniature to full-sized figure afloat
on wintery thermals,
surfing gusts in an effortless arc of descent
to hover above the mackerel on their beds of stinking ice,
his fine-boned face quizzical, impassive,
as he took in the stalls of brassicas and plums,

his bare and sinewy torso
kept aloft by imperceptible wing-beats
that turned to shushes when he corkscrewed suddenly upward
away over Henry Street and out toward the coastline,
his wings declining to a v, then a mote, then nothing,
a few seconds before you'd rounded the corner.

## Noel Monahan

BOG ENERGY

No walls here, a bog windwardly open
To hummocks and loughs where life floats,
Moss, the only building block, holds twenty
Times its weight in water. Tiny match-sticks
Stretch above the amber and brown, waiting
For the wind to set the sphagnum spores
On fire. Frogs croak, sedge quakes, curlews call for rain.
You'll find tenebrae down here in dreamless dark.
Wild heather opens a wet womb
That will pickle a body as soon as it's dropped.
The bog holds flesh on bone, hair
On heads. The Clonycavan man was raised
With gel in his hair, the Meenybradden woman
Found aflame in a dark ocean of turf.

Paula Bohince

THE MOOSE

Midnight in the White Mountains
means carousing in M's silver Jeep, which is
mostly air, air and psychedelic disco,
air and music and stars, unfolding maps
of stars overlapping, swirled thumbprint of
Milky Way, air and song
and constellations, going fast, when an owl swings
over the road I miss it, a kind of wind
here so strange they named an inn for it,
what is it called? A moose!
A moose straight ahead, the low beams
caught its handsome legs, like trees
furred, but all four sprang from a mother,
this moose fell the long route
to the ground and now he's
a grandfather in overalls, tall and behatted.
He moves like an ancient,
the bells of his hooves toll soundlessly,
the signal to move them must travel so far!
As in the days when an operator
placed a call for you and you waited
to be connected. Telephone calls
were exciting then, the moose is a call from
that era. It will rain soon, the flies will be
adolescents by morning. Time *flies*.
If only it was this velveteen animal,
moseying, no *moosying* the years
and the weathers. There is this moment,
our breathing and his, exhale
of the grasses he strides through,
it's as though he is being born again,
and we are the witnesses,
like the two Marys who knew Jesus and waited
for His return and saw His return,
how He looked almost through them, His
face already turning away, separate now
as He was from His earthly loves.

# Richard Murphy

## TRANSGRESSING INTO POETRY

*Six chapters from my work-in-progress, 'Transgressing into Poetry', appeared in PIR 104 and 107. The five chapters that follow are based on notes written in the process of giving voice in sonnet form to houses that speak directly or indirectly about their history and my life. A river of words was in full flood before and after the birth of my 'Natural Son' in the Rotunda Hospital on 29 January 1982. I was living in Killiney at 'Knockbrack', and a chapter with a sonnet of that title ends the work-in-progress. I dedicated* The Price of Stone *to Dennis O'Driscoll in 1985, and I thank Barbara Brown for her day by day e-mail critical encouragement of 'Transgressing into Poetry'.*

## CARLOW VILLAGE SCHOOLHOUSE

*Mon 11 Jan 1982*

> Not what you've done, but what you're going to do
> Matters now ...

Thanks to my father, who never owned a house till he built one on a farm in Rhodesia at the age of 63, because he spent so much on my private education, I may take for granted the comfort in which I live ... until a blizzard cuts the power lines, and returns me to fumbling by candlelight.

Strangers have often asked, 'How come your name is Murphy and you're not a Catholic?' A third-generation Irish American, who had never been to Ireland but hated Britain and my accent, shouted this question, silencing the crowd in a Kansas City bar called the Westport Inn late at night after a poetry reading in the Sixties. My host, a Professor of English called Ryan, bustled me out.

Renegade! Souper! Apostate! Jumper! Turncoat! Traitor! One of my forefathers, to survive starvation, may have earned these insults generations ago ... may have drunk the soup of Protestants to avoid starvation ... must have been taught to read the English Bible and stop speaking Irish.

Four years ago in Sydney I met a third cousin of mine who told me that our great-grandfather, Richard William Murphy, had a violent temper that ran in the family. Since before the famine of 1845-48, he had been the master of a Church of Ireland parish school in a small village called Nurney, Co Carlow. His infamous rage had provoked his eldest son, Edward, to sail to Australia, never to return; and his second son, my grandfather, also Richard William, to take refuge in Holy Orders.

So I drove to Nurney to enquire about that remote source of my own tendency to roar with anger, often at night in a fearful dream. There I met an old Church of Ireland farmer called Archie Smyth, whose mother had been the last teacher in the village school before it fell into ruin and was pulled down to widen the road. Murphy had left his name in local legend as an ogre of cruelty in the classroom. Archie told me:

> For each word of Irish uttered by a boy in school, a notch was cut on a tally-stick the boy had to wear round his neck as a collar of disgrace. I can show you the master's desk in the barn, you may take it if you like, but it's full of woodworm. There's a box on the side facing the children where he kept his freshly cut canes. When a boy was to be thrashed, he'd be carried on the back of another boy, who would hold his arms. That's the way things were in the past. The young today have no manners, no respect. They have it all too easy.

He showed me his mother's less intimidating desk with a sloping lid. Glued to the underside was a copy of the curriculum authorised by the Church Education Society for Ireland (founded in 1839) for the 'Male Scale of Proficiency'. Most important of all was the requirement to learn by heart long passages of the Bible selected by the Rector, who had lived in the house that now belonged to the farmer on the village square. Landlords had funded the Society as a bulwark against the Congregation of Christian Brothers in competing for the souls of the children of the poor. The Protestant way was to nourish their minds on the verbal manna of the Word of God in English.


*Tuesday 12 Jan 1982*

That change of language from Irish to English ... the daily reading of the Bible ... the Sunday singing of psalms and hymns in a mournful church ... 'change and decay in all around I see' ... enforced through five or six generations on their rise from bog-dens and sod-huts to houses like Milford and Lake Park ... stepping up from the class of servants to that of masters ... as the teacher was the first to do ... on the strength of his mind, his voice and his hand as demonstrated by his bold masculine signature, like my father's, clearly legible as a witness in a marriage register dated July 1845 ... when the blight was beginning to blacken the potato fields across Ireland ... that change of language ultimately gave me the voice with which I speak and write ... a voice that hungers for authority and yearns to make people and things, which are sure to vanish, last in verbal granite ... my lifelong transgression.

Try to give the schoolhouse a voice that speaks to you from the past in your mind, in your blood and in your style...

What do you expect to find in me? ... nothing is left but what you may find in yourself, tracing it back through generations of the same name ... the same temper ... the same deep fear of poverty ... on the long climb out of the clay ... women advancing men in marriages .

Do not be didactic, but give me a form that your conscience feels is true ... because I no longer exist to make a case for myself, unless revived by the force you get through your father's father from me. All that's left is a gap where I stood through famine after famine improving the minds of children in a village square. A school as formal and strict and poor as mine, two Irish miles down the road at Leighlinbridge, educated John Tyndall, a great scientist. I stood on one side of an octagon made by four handsome houses facing the centre of a crossroads near our steepled church, where the master led the choir, on a hilltop where potatoes were saved from the blight.

How angry my tenant was, how hungry his children, to gain and use the power of the written and spoken word, to free themselves from land they might till but never would own. For that big aggressive bullying man with a golden voice, who married above himself a draper's daughter, imposing discipline as formal and rigid as my classical façade, there could be no drifting back to the cabins of destitute submission, or the candle-power of rebellion easily quenched by the army and navy that stood loyal to the king.

But to be fair to him, fair to yourself, was it only the hunger of ambition, or ambition spurred by hunger, that drove him in using oppression not to be oppressed? ... he may have had your nature, your temper ... loved to make things clear ... hated the muddle, the mess, the blight, the mystification of people stuck in the clay, their superstition derived from erroneous fantastic thinking ... may have wanted reason to rescue him, and himself to use reason to rescue others, from superstition generated by extreme poverty ... to fill the blank spaces of a child's mind with knowledge as hard as well dressed masonry ... to pass the poetic mysteries of the Bible, together with the logic of mathematics, algebra and geometry, down through unimaginable generations for the benefit you enjoy at your desk today, putting words together with an inherited love of symmetry.

So be fair to him … without his love of learning and speaking lyrical passages of the English bible by heart, even if it *was* coercive and cruel, you'd not be writing this now … and has your own love of poetry never been tainted with coercion and cruelty?

It's not to be a poem about the famine, but about the power of the word in bringing people out of destitution into prosperity. Given occupancy of the schoolhouse, opposite the dispensary, and between the rectory and the rent office, his mind was influenced by the building's relation to other structures of power, having the same proportions as windows in mansions, though on a smaller scale. The schoolhouse, in which he lived upstairs, confirmed his desire for order, thrift, stability, status, and comfort, and it changed his life: it freed him from the pauperism of the bog-den, the sod-hut, the mud-cabin, the workhouse and the coffin ship; but it cut him off, by placing him inside its golden rectangular windows, from all the good poor Catholic people outside in the cold and wet.

CARLOW VILLAGE SCHOOLHOUSE

Much as you need a sonnet house to save
Your muse, while sifting through our foetid pits
Of blighted roots, he needed my firm, grave
Façade, to be freed from bog dens and sod huts.

Such symmetry he gained from me, you got
By birth, given his names. Twenty poor scholars,
Birched if they uttered Irish words, he taught
To speak like you, faults notched on wooden collars.

We faced the crossroads four square. Where I stood
Is void now, so be fair. Not forced to sip
The cauldron soup with undying gratitude,
Would you have chosen to board a coffin ship?

All you've seen is his proud clean signature
As a wedding witness that worst famine year.

*12 Jan 1982*

# FAMILY SEAT

*Tues 26 Jan 1982*

While waiting for my friend to give birth to our child, I keep hearing a
voice from the dead speaking of my mother's six maiden aunts at
Ballinamore House, between Kiltimach, Balla and Claremorris, with
three avenues, one going in each direction ... who lived unscathed
through the Troubles, when Anglo-Irish landlords were being shot or
their houses set on fire ... who clung to heirlooms through change and
decay ... Ormsby crested silver spoons, polished by servants, counted and
put away in velvet drawers ... a wind-up musical box that tinkles for an
hour ... a silver jug in the form of a cow that gives milk from its genteel
mouth ... relics of an empire reduced to a stamp collection in a library
where the chimney smokes and rain batters the golden rectangular
windows, their sash cords fraying ... with a view of hills across an invisible
ha-ha, if it's not raining ... the voice of a once powerful house-cum-family
in terminal decline.

Now when walls are being pulled down and bungalows put up in parks
of the old demesnes, why am I still writing sonnets? It could be because
the ingrown need for what has been lost goes on ... the sonnets are my
hexagon, my beehive cell, my folly, and my walled garden ... which deprive
no one of land they need to live on, keep nobody out, can be overrun,
and not go to seed ... a scent of lime flowers and the hum of bees ... a
taste of buttermilk from a wooden churn ... glimpse of a woodcock's
long curved beak sticking out of a game-bag ... and the sound of horses
dragging a mowing machine in diminishing circles round and around a
field of oats that men and women are binding with wisps of straw.

So as not to confuse them, let the Ballinamore poem, with an upholstered
title such as 'Family Seat', deal with the orderly oppressiveness, boredom,
and propriety of the demesne ... the failure to marry and have children ...
the fossilisation of feelings in property ... subjugation of servants in the
basement ... so that a Milford poem, perhaps called 'Birth Place', may deal
with the demesne's profusion, decadence and generosity ... the subversion
of order by my loveable artistic Milford grandmother's uncontrollable
black Labrador dogs.
 Ballinamore was a formidable house with a face of disapproval ...
built to dominate a vast estate of poor land acquired by conquest and
marriages ... where feelings were turned to stone by a house that had
consumed its hereditary owners' love ... giving them back a wealth of

lovely things ... the sonnet might conclude with the Protestant 'Family Seat' converted, as it was in 1935, by the St John of God nuns into a home for the paralysed in body or in mind.

*Sat 30 Jan1982*

In helping my friend to have the child she wanted, a son born yesterday in the Rotunda under the sign of Aquarius, in all the difficulties of our unmarried situation and what she loathes about my split-level life, we have had to endure the disapproval of our families, which the sonnet 'Family Seat' will be about ... that enclosed propriety ... that legitimacy of the landed proprietor with his law of primogeniture, and his preference for marrying his cousin to keep the property in the family ... that possession of people by the things they own ... and that ownership of each other which makes me feel imprisoned ... and a fear that the offspring may turn out to be some kind of monster ... or die in childhood, as did the first five children of my mother's Miller grandmother, who married her Ormsby of Ballinamore cousin at sixteen.

NATURAL SON

Before the spectacled professor snipped
The cord, I heard your birth-cry flood the ward,
And lowered your mother's tortured head, and wept.
The house you'd left would need to be restored.

No worse pain could be borne, to bear the joy
Of seeing you come in a slow dive from the womb
Pushed from your fluid home, pronounced 'a boy'.
You'll never find so well-equipped a room.

No house we build could hope to satisfy
Every small need, now that you've made this move
To share our loneliness, much as we try
Our vocal skill to wall you round with love.

This day you crave so little, we so much
For you to live, who need our merest touch.

*31 Jan 1982*

*Mon 1 Feb 1982*

Dennis [O'Driscoll], on the phone, thinks 'Natural Son' provides 'a master key to the sonnet houses ... a statement by the poet speaking in his own voice instead of ventriloquising'.

FAMILY SEAT

Clouds make me look as though I disapprove
Of everyone. You know that grim, grey face
Of limestone cut by famine workmen. Love
Is never allowed to show it rules the place

But love I took from a ruling family
And gave them back a wealth of lovely things:
As a trout river talking with propriety
Through cockshoot woods, bailiffed by underlings.

Their silver knives adored their crested forks.
Blue-veiny hands, like yours, kept my clocks wound
On endless landings: others did good works
Like typing braille. High walls surround my land.

They've all been buried in their name-proud vaults,
Paraplegics live here now, and love my faults.

*1 Feb 1982*


HEXAGON

*Fri 10 Sept 1982, 11 p.m.*

Resolution renewed in the dark at the Folly on Killiney Hill. Lights of the city extending from Howth to Bray Head in a broad, broken curve. Friday night in the pubs. Hectic enjoyment. Cleggan far away. The sequence in my mind. Too much food at dinner. Heartburn. Teenagers dancing to rock music in a corrugated iron shed under dark stately trees. Raucous and violent sounds of a capital city. Not mine, though I live here, apart.

Alone at Knockbrack tonight ... listening to Mozart's *Clarinet Quintet* ... remembering Tony [White] doing carpentry at the Hexagon on Omey,

the holy island you can walk to, or escape from, when the tide is low ...
remembering Tony's death in London six months later.

Stay in Dublin until the sonnet sequence is finished ... perhaps fifty ...
no entertainment, no news, and no engagements until this is done ...
keep filling the notebook with ideas for sonnet dwellings.

*Sun 12 Sept 1982*

Move ahead, now, with the reconstruction in verse of that ideal building,
the Hexagon, behind and above Omey's graveyard ... perched on an
outcrop of rock ... walls of dressed and undressed granite salvaged from
ruins of cabins that once may have housed families of ten children but
now are considered unfit for cattle ... a house of one room contained in a
single honeycomb cell ... achieving concentricity ... six angles described
by a circle ... five views and a wall with books above one bed ... shelves
for a hundred books ... a number Tony thought enough for anyone to
keep ... and the 'Bookcase for the *OED*' he built of Parana pine to fit at
the foot of my bed ... which he made of oak planks from Cong Forest ...
everything fitting without being cramped ... hexagonal table of teak on a
granite base supporting the centre of a flat roof with a pole ... tongued
and grooved ceiling-boards fixed in a pattern of hexagons widening board
by board from the centre ... giving me whenever I come from outside
and close the door a feeling of calm centripetal force.

Arms of the sea embrace the island twice a day, always a little later
and later, governed by the moon, cutting me off, as I need to be cut off
from wasteful distractions to concentrate ... alone here in a cell, like a
hermit, or a hermit crab ... a pagan cell for the cult of poetry ... with a
picture window looking down a long green cleft to a lake with a border
of reeds and a flock of wild swans ... and above the lake a cliff occupied
by choughs and a pair of merlins ... who, when they fly, are tormented by
a gaggle of tatterdemalion jackdaws ... and beyond all this a vision of
High Island on the horizon.

Through a window facing east, I can see Claddaghduff Church on
the mainland ... funeral processions crossing the strand at walking speed
to the Omey graveyard, a few fields away but out of sight from the
Hexagon ... grave of Tony's ashes and mine to come. For five hours,
while the strand is closed by the sea, I can stay secure from the wind and
the slanting rain, the disturbance of visitors, and my own temptation to
return to the mainland ... enjoying a spring tide of inspiration ... a gift
from the honeycomb's concentricity ... Tony's last gift of his carpentry,
his craft and his mind ... well made for the whorling of sonnet shells that
may be ground to sand on a critical beach.

A vision difficult to sustain and always under a threat. As soon as the
roof was watertight, an order was issued by the Planning Authority of

the Galway County Council to pull the Hexagon down ... 'impairing the visual amenity of the landscape' ... though I had designed the stone cell to look as if it had grown out of the rock on which it stood ... 'rupestral' ... as I told the District Judge in Clifden Court, who dismissed the case with costs against the Council. Much later, when I saw a neighbour's cattle, herded by his dog, smash through my barbed wire fence on which he had put a 'NO TRESPASSING' sign, I gave up trying to write there ... built a granite studio in my garden in Cleggan, with no views except of evergreen hedges ... had to sell the Hexagon to pay for this ... the price of my love of stone.

Bright days slipping away like clover seed through my fingers. I miss a sunset to repair a fence. 'Come to me before the closing of the strand', I write to a friend, 'and be in my bed when the tide reaches high water'. Come in from the wild night and smell the baking of bread ... small hiss of gas light over a plain pine desk ... a moth has settled on the spine of The Faerie Queene ... serenity of soul in the hexagon ... but at my back I hear a lonely sound of the wind wandering around the corners of the hut, sighing and whistling like a friend shut out.

A vision that imposes order flows out across the land and seascape that are wild ... the wildness flows back into the order of the hexagon ... this contrary, simultaneous current is like the tide ... in and out ... this concerns me writing a sonnet ... how to balance the destroyer against the creator who needs to destroy in order to create ... the ruins that supplied the stone to build the Hexagon ... the trees felled in a forest to provide timber for bookshelves and roof ... the wildcat entering through a window at night and ravaging my dream.

*Thur 16 Sep 1982*

Six or seven years ago, when I sat in a black armchair in the Hexagon, with a fountain pen in my hand and the sun pouring over my shoulder, the page was sometimes too bright to look at, the view of wild swans on a lake too nearly a poem someone else had written, the composition of art and nature achieved ... my shell encompassed me ... why bother to write? I could look out on a corner of the world I loved, from the shelter of a granite carapace, and ignore what I feared or hated elsewhere...

But is that true?

Sometimes I was discontented on my own, turning to pick up the binoculars and see who might be walking across the beach towards the island ... or look to the west at a graveyard long disused, where only women were buried on a hillock of sand above St Fechin's ancient church ... or down by the shore where the sea had cast up the skull of an infant buried in unconsecrated ground ... often I kept an eye on a rock on the beach to reckon how long I could stay before a rising tide would close the strand...

The Hexagon was designed for a contemplative life I seldom lived ... I built it as a dream, but was forced to sell it three years later for a song.

HEXAGON

Three watchful openings of clear plate glass
Give you command of a stormy desolate view
From my hilltop sundial cell as you look across
Dunes, rocks and sea to islands west of Omey.

Six random walls round one all purpose room
Of calm rupestral concentricity,
With a smell of yeast bread flowering, enwomb
Your pride in the hermit hut you made of me.

Oak bed, a hundred books, a staunch teak door
And the Twelve Pins of your childhood I include.
No need for you to write. Sun and moon pore
Over curled up fly leaves, brilliantly intrude.

Flood tide, closing the strand, comes to embrace
Our isolation. Blue arms interlace.

*19 Sept 1982*

NEW FORGE

*13-20 Oct 1982*

Now to the New Forge ... a house that embedded me in Connemara for thirteen years ... built by my neighbours in Cleggan after my father died. He had spent most of his life in resplendent British colonies, while I chose to live under clouds among Irish Catholic nationalists near his and my mother's roots ... on the ocean edge of his father's desolate Church of Ireland parish of Omey. The shock of his death confirmed my desire to build a house of local granite ... where poetry could make rubble fragments of my life integral as random stones in a course of masonry ... stone bonded by stone.

Warm pink to dark red colours of the granite ruins of cottages dating back to the famine in our neighbourhood reminded me of the walls of a tavern in a small Breton fishing village, where shortly after Patricia and I had met as mature students in Paris, she brought me to stay in the gloom and gales of December 1954 ... the wine was dark and rough as the sea ... in a bus on our way to Concarneau in the rain we agreed to marry. Wanting, after my father died in 1965, to build a better house in Cleggan, where I was living up a narrow lane behind the Pier Bar in a cottage called the Old Forge, I found and bought the granite of seven ruins ... saving it from burial in foundations of new roads. The widowed mother of my mates Owen and Seamus Coyne on the Ave Maria and the True Light gave me a site next to the forge garden commanding an easterly view over the village and across Cleggan Bay as far as the Diamond Mountain above Letterfrack. A Scottish architect, James Shearer, with roots in Dunfermline and a London practice, who chartered the True Light for a family holiday each August, designed the house fulfilling my wish for the façade to reconcile the rootedness of an Irish cottage with the elegance of an Anglo-Irish house in a demesne. Our mason, John Cosgrove, modelled his dry stonework on the style of an early Celtic oratory.

All this detail will not fit in a sonnet ... too much rain on a mountain turns a waterfall into a gush ... but memories need to be refreshed before a few may be channelled and compressed into sonnet form.

The walls of my new house in Cleggan rose while I was a guest for two months at the Colonnade Club on the Lawn of the University designed by Jefferson in Charlottesville, Virginia. Before the house was roofed with sea-green slates from Cumbria, Ted Hughes, who was staying with Assia and the children at Cleggan Farm across the bay, had suggested calling it the New Forge. For ten years I enjoyed living there, feeling that now I belonged in a house that belonged to me ... the rock and shell of my forged identity as a poet ... where I finished *The Battle of Aughrim* followed by *High Island* ... until shaken by the sudden death in February 1976 of Tony White ... and in September the following year Patricia's suicide.

Here at Knockbrack, a flimsy house on granite foundations, I have tried to sublimate my passion for building into the making of sonnets ... often harassed by the labour ... and the paradox that inspiration cannot be forced, nor will it flow without work ... so now I must labour to vocalise the building that became a carapace I had to shed to grow.

After putting the New Forge in the hands of a Dublin auctioneer, I felt vulnerable as a crayfish coming out of its barnacled shell ... there's a technical word for this process – exuviate – which sounds just as awkward as its meaning ... when rain lashed the walls that sheltered me in the house, the granite glowed like the shell of a crayfish in a wicker pot hauled from the seabed on to a deck ... I loved that house but I had to move ... never to be integral again but to grow more articulate with age ... so 'New Forge' will be a poem of metamorphosis, from stone into poetry. There were many obstacles to selling in 1979 ... a strike cutting off our telephone and mail for four months, no petrol for two, no bids at an auction except off the wall ... until chance brought a large family from Wicklow on holiday to Cleggan in July ... who, seeing a red granite gable rising above 'pleasure ground' garden walls with a sign reading HOUSE FOR SALE, bought into a dream from which I was waking. But when they woke from their dream, after schools for their eight children reopened in September, they leased the house for a peppercorn rent to the Brothers of Charity, who ran a home for the mentally handicapped in Clarenbridge.

Since then, the New Forge, designed for writing poetry under an attic skylight above an oasis of books in a desert of literacy, has been changed into a weekend retreat for men with the minds of toddlers ... why? ... because failures caused by my folly in split-heartedness compelled me to obey the haunting injunction of Rilke, 'You must change your life.'

Leaving the west and settling in south county Dublin gave me the stimulus of conversation with poets and critics. Finding a house that faced mountains and turned its back to the sexually liberated city, whose lights beckoned in the ten miles distant dark, gave me freedom to write poems of displacement and estrangement set in the modern world ... exposed to the city's moral radiation.

But how strong the pressure of Connemara to bring me back to where I was deeply implanted ... even this morning on my run in the dark before dawn to the top of Killiney Hill and around the Folly clockwise I thought of offering the buyers a bargain if they would exchange the New Forge for Knockbrack ... umbilical cordite.

Predators around a crevice ... waiting for the carapace to be shed ... starlings infesting shrubbery at nightfall ... brain-damaged men filling the vacated shell with nonsensical noise ... trampling heather and rue from Slieve Donard across the border ... twittering of ghosts in my ear on a pillow.

Random stone laid without mortar in regular courses gives most musical pleasure to the eye ... with crevices deep enough for blue tits to nest in safety between the stones ... sparkle of mica in a sunbeam on granite after rain ... stone bonded by stone making symmetry out of fragments ... alternative housing for ambiguous needs ... in a crevice or on a crag.

From derelict huts of Cleggan rock I grew
To look most natural here, though I began
Strangely; your Breton stone design drawn through
A London architect's Dunfermline plan.

For thirteen years this perfect place to write
Creviced you in my Galway garden bond;
Green Cumbrian slates letting in attic light;
Slieve Donard heather's white cross border stand.

Why did you sell me? Did you feel trapped here,
Compelled in cold blood to exuviate
My hard pink shell? A Dublin auctioneer
Hammered you free to grow articulate.

Our union was split level. Now I'm used
To keep old men with infant minds amused.

*Wed 20 Oct 1982*


## KNOCKBRACK

*May – Nov 1983*

The best and worst news in the same week ... the American Irish
Foundation gives me an award of $10,000 for poetry written long ago ...
and my son is taken away by his mother, for good reasons, never to be
brought back. What next?

Perhaps it's time to let the house where the sonnets have been written
speak ... where I'm writing now, in the last house at the dead end of the
twists and turns of a lovers' lane ... a sad-looking house when I saw it
first, where nobody had stayed long ... where I've spent more than two
years trying to make poems that will last ... never mind if they're
forgotten ... their making is what matters ... so let 'Knockbrack' have the
final word as the colophon of a book beginning with 'Folly'.

Remember and reinvent ... house hunting in Dublin ... feeling homeless
and scared after selling my house in the west where my best poetry had

been written ... guilty of having a load of money I was afraid of losing ... not knowing whether to live in Dublin or London, but sure I needed to dispossess myself of the New Forge ... where, after thirteen years protected by high garden walls, I had begun to feel entombed.

A week after the money reached my account, searching in South County Dublin, I drove down a gravel lane that ended at a sign ... HOUSE FOR SALE ... but no sign of a house ... only a weather-beaten caravan, painted chocolate and cream, parked in a muddy space almost too narrow for a car to turn ... beyond that a bosky wilderness.

Lured by an arrow nailed to a Scots Fir, I climbed a path lined with blue agapanthus, the flower of love, a colonial intruder ... and entered a mysterious covert of Bourbon roses, myrtle, laburnum and silver birch ... so quiet that the distant sirens of police cars and ambulances sounded like faintly dissonant music on a ground of birdsong and silence ... ideal setting for a small Edwardian cottage whose faults appealed to the builder in me to put right ... above the house, grey granite rose in outcrops from beds of golden whins ... a reclusive site with its back to the city ten miles away and its face to the mountains across the Vale of Shanganagh ... reminiscent of a T'ang dynasty poem I had enjoyed in translation.

Hundreds of buyers had viewed the place and turned it down ... partly for the cost of its renovation, but more for the loneliness of a misshapen house of eclectic privacy accessible only on foot from a lane unlit at night ... perhaps frequented by drug addicts or burglars. The English owners were selling because they were afraid to let their children walk home on the lane at night ... and the teenage son of a previous owner had died of exposure having collapsed in some nearby bushes while tripping on drugs. Though repelled by its name, 'Far Hills', I bought the place quickly, before losing all my money in a worse speculation.

While wanting to give the place a better name, I found it had first been called 'The Whins' by the famous Dublin bookseller, Willie Figgis, of Hodges Figgis and Co., who had built a cottage here in time for his honeymoon. When I was nineteen, and wanted to write poetry, that learned gentleman, who had known my father as a student at Trinity College Dublin, had allowed me to browse among the rare books locked in a cabinet in his back room, and to buy for next to nothing an uncut copy of Yeats's *New Poems* published by the Cuala Press in 1938. But I didn't want to live in a suburban house called 'The Whins'.

Between the First and Second World Wars, 'The Whins' was occupied by a tall religious devotee with a long dark beard who is said to have written poetry. Uplifted by the glory of the International Eucharistic Congress of 1932 in Dublin, he had walked barefoot through England, France and Italy to Rome. In honour of the Virgin Mary, he had changed the name of the house to 'Maryknoll'. Then a Protestant businessman, having bought the house for the view across the Killiney golf course, called it 'Far Hills'.

I thought the name 'Knockbrack' would be appropriate for a speckled hill of gorse, heather and granite, linking me to the townland where I had last lived in the west. But when I asked John McGahern for advice, he put me down by saying he would prefer, if the house were his, to use its postal number.

The house had many faults ... lead pipes leaking with age and a lead-lined tank, poisoning the water supply ... casement windows with broken diamond-shaped leaded panes ... easy for burglars to enter ... expensive if not impossible to repair ... frames rotting under a recent coat of paint ... a wooden roof covered by green mineral felt that could catch fire from sparks of bush-fires lit by smokers on the wild windward side of the garden ... picture windows in recent extensions disjointing the proportions and clashing with the look of the old leaded casements.

So I hired workmen who were living on the dole... they dug out a wrought iron pergola, felled a laburnum that reminded me of Baymount, where the boys had made me terrified of the poison in its pods ... removed 'Beauty Board' that was covering the dampness of walls to deceive a buyer ... installed copper pipes and a zinc tank ... while a company directed by the gloriously titled Macgillicuddy of the Reeks altered the windows to keep them in proportion with double-glazed units of anodised aluminium framed in mahogany.

The Dublin tradesmen disappointed me by taking less pride in their work than the Connemara men who had built the New Forge, the Hexagon and the Miners' Hut. If I complained about poor quality, they would say, 'You won't notice when the job is finished'. But I did notice when the corridor flooded because six months earlier a carpenter had driven a nail through a floor into a new copper pipe.

The fear that makes me want to keep out burglars and drug addicts clashes with a perverse desire to invite them to come in ... my forlorn search for the love of a young man has caused me to reject the love of a woman who loves me too much ... neat sentences woven on a web of desperation.

This really happened, but I'll tell it as if it were a dream, because the reality remains present in my mind as a nightmare of an encounter in the twilight on a corner of the lane below my house ... when walking back from the Folly I suddenly came face to face with a tall young man ... short hair, black jeans, leather jacket ... unsteady on his feet, he holds out his hand for me to shake and says, in a doleful accent,

'Long time no see ... don't you remember? ... me and my friends took tadpoles from your ponds up there ... and you gave us apple juice.'

'You've grown since then, but I think I remember you.'

'I've been away ... done six months for grievous bodily harm.'

Grinning, he milks my thumb ... seems unaware of giving me provocative pleasure bordering on pain.

'Were you the boy with no father or mother who was reared by his aunt?'

'Too true!'

'Did one of your gang tell me you were the second best fighter in the school?'

'Correct! Bùt I soon became the best.'

Increasing the pressure on my thumb, he brings his face close to mine and stares in my eyes so hard that he frightens me ... perhaps he'll break my nose with a head-butt ...from ear to ear on his neck I notice a horrible scar ... he boasts,

'My best friend pulled a knife on me in an argument and a doctor gave me a hundred and twenty stitches.'

His grip on my thumb and his lean body, swaying in front of me like a hooded king cobra, cause me to tremble ... lust fuelled by fear ... dare I ask him up to my house, taking a lunatic risk? ... but his lunacy saves me from mine as he solemnly declares,

'I can see in your eyes you have cancer and will soon be dead ... I said the same about my aunt, who reared me from the age of two, and she died within a month ... there's no use denying it, man, I can see death in your eyes ... you might last three months, no longer ... after that you'll be dead as my aunt in her grave at the Deans Grange Cemetery ... the Lord have mercy upon her ... I hated the cunt.'

Then, loosening the screw of his fingers on my thumb, he staggers down a path into a thicket of briars and blackthorn ... while I flee up the newly tarred drive to the house ... as I fumble the key in the lock of my front door, I hear his raucous bass voice from the bushes laughing and shouting,

'You queer old fucker ... ha ha ha ... you will soon be dead.'

No child has been born at Knockbrack, nor did I let my newly born son live here with his mother, because they might have disturbed the writing they inspired. Great shame in this choice ... against nature but not against mine. They have gone, now, and I can't wish them back. The boy will grow up not knowing and not wanting to know his father.

On returning here, summer or winter, autumn or spring, I feel, often with relief but sometimes with dismay, there is nowhere further to go ... the road has come to an end ... beyond this I must transcend myself on an inward journey alone through a crowd of memories ... writing with a fountain pen on a page lined with centimetre squares ... word after word

on a quest that often fails to achieve a poem ... or else the road will seem
to have led me down a blind alley.

Now I want to build a poem that will be beyond repair ... concerning a
house that needed much repairing ... composed of extensions,
improvements and mistakes of previous owners ... to house my feelings
in the voice of a poem that will be no more than indirectly mine ...
composed of the sounds of many voices I have heard and read throughout
my life ... as I try not to be overawed into silence on one hand or falsely
transgressive on another ... while daring, without the talent or the genius,
being no more than a poetic handyman, to adapt a structure perfected by
consummate sonneteers.


KNOCKBRACK

When driven to explore a strange blind alley
First clambering footloose up a speckled hill
You gambled on rare views of infilled valley,
Blossom of Chinese tang on a thorny grill.

Coming to speculate, you stayed for good:
Your fortune in the gold market of whins.
Avuncular pines admonished you to brood
On dark tale ends with woodcut colophons.

A spirited father walked barefoot to Rome:
A son died sniffing glue. Nobody lasted.
Well finished as rifle bolts at the Somme
My door locks made you feel safely invested.

Grey granite cropped up an archaic head
To check your feet, your line of living dead.

*11 Nov 1983*

Peter Sirr

## THE PLEASURE GROUND

Richard Murphy, *Poems 1952–2012* (The Lilliput Press, 2013), €15.

Richard Murphy's poems have been a solid fixture in Irish poetry for so long that it's all too easy to take the achievement for granted. But it's worth being regularly reminded of a poetic output which, even if it hasn't been added to substantially for twenty years, still raises its imposing bulk like a craggy Atlantic rock. This handsome volume again lays out the work that made and sustained his reputation since it first started to appear in the 1960s. Probably the most definitive early poem is 'Sailing to an Island', which also provided the title for his first collection. It sets the characteristic classicism of the style with what would become typical Murphy concerns: man's struggle with elemental nature, the harsh life of the western seaboard, the masculine energies of boat-building, sailing and poem making. 'Sailing to an Island' pits its narrator against the sea and near-disaster yet brings him safely in its solidly iambic craft to shelter and home. Other poems like 'The Cleggan Disaster' and 'The Last Galway Hooker' are rooted in the same tradition – the latter makes an explicit identification between the restoration of a boat and the impulse to write that is lodged 'in memory's hands'.

These early poems are brilliant verbal performances, line building on line in a way Seamus Heaney, thinking of how the timbers of a *púcán* are laid, described as 'clinker-built'. 'Wittgenstein and the Birds' is a typical example:

> He clipped with February shears the dead
> Metaphysical foliage. Old, in fieldfares
> Fantasies rebelled though annihilated.
>
> He was haunted by gulls beyond omega shade,
> His nerve tormented by terrified knots
> In pin-feathered flesh ...

There is the sense of the careful weighting of word and phrase, the formality and poise of the diction, the wrought-iron enjambment. Yet as you read the poems you realise how flexible is the instrument that builds them – the perfect tool for narrative. And storytelling is one of the chief engines of the poems, a kind of narrative putting of the houses of family, memory and legacy in order, as in 'The Woman of the House':

On a patrician evening in Ireland
I was born in the guest room: she delivered me.
May I deliver her from the cold hand
Where now she lies, with a brief elegy?

Murphy's Anglo-Irish heritage fuels the interest in history and colonial
conflict that comes most strongly to the fore in the extended sequence
'The Battle of Aughrim'. Wanting to understand, as he puts it himself
'the borders and bigotries', the 'devastations and divisions in myself as
well as Ireland', the poet attempts a wide camera sweep of the entire
action, spanning the present and past, juxtaposing the personal and the
historical, the post-colonial state and the tangled history it emerged
from. It's a vividly realised dramatic poem whose most memorable
moments are not the battle itself or even the vanity and treachery of some
of the main players like St Ruth and Luttrell, but the suffering of
individual victims: the killing of a captured boy, the hanging of an
innocent couple, the anxiety of a planter, the apprehension of a dragoon
on the eve of combat.

What's striking about the poem is its reportorial exactness as well as
the even-handed splintering of its perspective amongst the various
participants, an act of sympathetic imagination which is at the core of
Murphy's achievement.

The poems tend always to have this surface coolness: the passion is in
the craft, in the chiselled perfection with its stone-like density. The teller,
the poet, is always there in the background tapping away, a subdued but
unmistakable presence. The bravura effect of the craft comes through in
all its theatricality in a poem like 'Seals at High Island' which from its
arresting opening to its mournful end is a wonderfully orchestrated
series of set-pieces:

The calamity of seals begins with jaws.
Born in caverns that reverberate
With endless malice of the sea's tongue
Clacking on shingle, they learn to bark back
In fear and sadness and celebration.
The ocean's mouth opens forty feet wide
And closes on a morsel of their rock.

Murphy is most at ease in the elemental world of nature and the struggle
to live with it. His is very much a poetry of place, but of place – whether
Connemara or the Ceylon of his childhood – seen from the outside in.
The careful observation and immaculate construction have the outsider's
sense of detail and the outsider's detachment. They are a kind of

negotiation of the distance his heritage put between him, the public school and Oxford-educated son of a colonial administrator, and his chosen place and people. The emotional and aesthetic distance is crucial; much of the drama springs from learning to be in a place, attempting to belong, or teaching others necessary skills, – how to read, or hold a scythe – and dealing with the losses that ensue – the death of a goat, an obsession with building so that the friends he neglects now might be entertained in the future which might never come. Some of the best poems, such as those about Tony White, are about other outsider-insiders, those who have abandoned the temptations of the city or modernity for a reduction to essentials, learning to live 'at the hub and not the rim / Of time'.

The formal detachment and the meticulousness of the craft shouldn't be mistaken for a lack of passion. The poems are full of feeling – their elaborate architecture is precisely a means of containing and articulating powerful emotions. This is perhaps most evident in 'The Price of Stone', a sonnet sequence in which each poem ventriloquises a building that has a resonance for the poet. This in turn means that the poet becomes the addressee, the biographical subject matter displaced into the consciousness of a roof-tree, restaurant or public convenience. They are free to address and accuse the poet so that the sequence also functions as an oblique self-examination. 'By making the persona of each sonnet the spirit of that house or structure,' the poet said in a recent interview, 'I found I was better able to transmute the mud of remembered experience into urns of poetry.' In these poems Murphy's is a mind in search of strategies to protect itself against its own privacy. Abhorring confessionalism, he can let his buildings do the dirty conscience work for him. It's a strange, and strangely effective achievement: cool, orderly, 'in granite style', seemingly remote yet full of quiet surprises, rhyming 'firmament' and 'ferment' but also 'steam' and 'jism', and ranging over a wide terrain, from the intimate to the declamatory, the pompous swagger to the bleak cruelty of Letterfrack Industrial School.

In that same interview Murphy talks of remembering, when distracted, Yeats's stricture to 'Hammer your thoughts into unity.' But he also remembered T S Eliot remarking to Harold Nicholson in the 1950s: 'Tell your friend Murphy that poetry is song.' His life's work fulfils the promise of both those commands: on the one hand the hammered and highly burnished, on the other his own unforgettable music.

Poems 1952-2012 is also published by Bloodaxe Books, as The Pleasure Ground: Poems 1952-2012

## Notes on Contributors

**Chris Agee** is the author of *In the New Hampshire Woods* (Dedalus Press, 1992), *First Light* (Dedalus Press, 2003) and *Next to Nothing* (Salt Publishing, 2009), the latter shortlisted for the 2010 Ted Hughes Award for New Work in Poetry, funded by the Poet Laureate and organised by the Poetry Society in London. He is the Editor of *Irish Pages*, and currently the Keith Wright Literary Fellow at the University of Strathclyde, Glasgow.

**Jacob Agee** was born in Belfast in 1993, attended St Michael's Primary School from 1997-2004 and the Royal Belfast Academical Institution ('Inst') from 2004-2011, and is now in his second year at Trinity College, Dublin, studying for a joint honours BA in Classics with Jewish and Islamic Civilisation. This is his first poem to be published in any journal.

**Jeffrey Alfier** has work appearing or forthcoming in *Connecticut Review*, *The South Carolina Review* and *New York Quarterly*. His latest chapbook is *The City Without Her* (Kindred Spirit Press, 2012) and his full-length book of poems, *The Wolf Yearling*, was published in 2013 by Pecan Grove Press.

**Sujata Bhatt** was born in India and grew up there and in the USA. She received her MFA from the Writers' Workshop at the University of Iowa. She is the author of six collections of poetry, a *Selected Poems* and a *Collected Poems*, all from Carcanet Press. The poems in this issue are from her new collection, *Poppies in Translation*, forthcoming in 2014. She has received numerous prizes including the Commonwealth Poetry Prize and a Cholmondeley Award. She divides her time between Germany and elsewhere.

**Paula Bohince** is the author of the poetry collections *The Children* (2012) and *Incident at the Edge of Bayonet Woods* (2008), both from Sarabande Books. Her poems have appeared in *The New Yorker*, *The New York Review of Books*, *The Irish Times*, and elsewhere. She lives in the USA.

**Eavan Boland** is Mabury Knapp Professor in Humanities and Director of the Creative Writing Program at Stanford University. Her *New Selected Poems* was published earlier this year by Carcanet Press.

**Matthew Brennan** has published poems and criticism in many journals, including the *The New York Times Book Review* and *The Sewanee Review*. He has published four collections of poetry, most recently *The House with The Mansard Roof* (The Backwaters Press, 2009). He lives in Indiana, USA.

**Marianne Burton's** pamphlet *The Devil's Cut* was a Poetry Book Society Choice. 'The Persistence of Vision' appears in her début collection, *She Inserts The Key*, published this year by Seren Books.

**Paddy Bushe** – see page 95.

**David Butler's** poetry collection *Via Crucis* was published by Doghouse Books in 2011. *No Greater Love*, a short story collection, was recently brought out by Ward Wood Publishing. New Island Press published his novel *The Judas Kiss* in 2012, and will publish the novel *City of Dis* early next year.

**Peter Carpenter's** *New and Selected Poems: Just Like That* was published by Smith/Doorstop in 2012; his chapter on creative writing ('Singing Schools and Beyond') appears in the *Handbook of Contemporary British and Irish Poetry* (Oxford University Press, 2013). He co-edits Worple Press (**www.worplepress.co.uk**).

**Liam Carson** is Director of the IMRAM Irish Language Literature Festival. He is the author of *Call Mother A Lonely Field*, published in Ireland by Hag's Head Press (2010) and in the UK by Seren Books (2012).

**Philip Coleman** teaches in the School of English, Trinity College, Dublin, where he specialises in American literature. He is the co-editor of *Reading Pearse Hutchinson: from Findrum to Fisterre* (Irish Academic Press, 2011). His book *John Berryman's Public Vision: Relocating 'the scene of disorder'* is forthcoming from UCD Press.

**Eamon Cooke** is a member of Boyne Writers Group and has placed poems recently in *Boyne Berries*, *The Stony Thursday Book* and *Force 10*. His collection *Berry Time* was published by Dedalus Press in 2002.

**Ross Donlon** (**www.rossdonlon.com**) is an Australian poet who has won a number of international poetry competitions and spoken word events. He has read at festivals in Australia, the Wenlock Poetry Festival in England, and in Galway and Cork in 2012. Extracts from his latest book, *The Blue Dressing Gown* (Profile Poetry, 2011), have been produced for national radio in Australia.

**Martina Evans** is an Irish poet and novelist. Her fourth poetry collection, *Facing the Public*, was published by Anvil Press in 2009. A *TLS* Book of the Year, *Facing the Public* received the Piero Ciampi International Poetry Prize in 2011. Her full-length prose poem, *Petrol*, a recipient of a Grants for the Arts Award, was published by Anvil Press in 2012.

**Diane Fahey** was selected for the 2013 Australian Poetry Tour of Ireland. She has won various poetry awards including the ACT government's Judith Wright Prize. *The Wing Collection: New and Selected Poems* was published in 2011 by Puncher & Wattmann.

**David Gardiner** lives in Chicago. From 2006–2010 he was founding editor of the international arts journal, *An Sionnach*. He was professor at Creighton University and Trinity College, Dublin, and visiting scholar at Boston College, New York University and the University of Ulster. He is currently guest poetry editor of *Burning Bush 2* (Dublin). His most recent poetry publication is *Downstate* (Salmon Poetry, 2011). 'These Dark Places' is from his forthcoming collection, *The Chivalry of Crime*.

**Matthew Geden** was born and brought up in the English Midlands, moving to Kinsale, Co Cork, in 1990. His second full-length poetry collection, *The Place Inside*, was published by Dedalus Press in 2012.

**Kerry Hardie** has published six collections of poetry with Gallery Press, her most recent being *The Ash and the Oak and the Wild Cherry Tree* (2012). Her *Selected Poems* was published by Gallery Press / Bloodaxe Books in 2011. She has also published two novels and is still trying to finish a third. She is a member of Aosdána.

**James Harpur** has had five collections of poetry published by Anvil Press. His latest volume, *Angels and Harvesters*, was a Poetry Book Society Recommendation and was shortlisted for the 2013 *Irish Times* Poetry Prize.

**Francis Harvey**'s published collections include *Collected Poems* (2007) and most recently *Donegal Haiku* (2013), both from Dedalus Press. His work has appeared in numerous magazines. He is a member of Aosdána.

**Andrew Hudgins** – see page 75.

**Neil Jordan**'s literary work includes *Night in Tunisia, The Past, The Dream of a Beast, Shade* and *Mistaken*. He film credits as writer-director include *The Company of Wolves, Mona Lisa, Interview with the Vampire* (screenplay by Anne Rice), *The Butcher Boy, Michael Collins* and *The Crying Game*, for which he won an Oscar for Best Screenplay.

**John Kinsella**'s most recent book of poetry, *Jam Tree Gully* (WW Norton, 2012), won the Australian Prime Minister's Award for Poetry in 2013. He is a Fellow of Churchill College, Cambridge University, and a Professorial Research Fellow at the University of Western Australia. He is currently spending time in Co Cork.

Michael Longley's poetry collection *Gorse Fires* (1991) won the Whitbread Poetry Prize, while *The Weather in Japan* (2000) won the T S Eliot Prize and the Hawthornden Prize. He was appointed Commander of the Order of the British Empire in 2010. His collection *A Hundred Doors* won the Poetry Now Award in September 2012.

Daniel Lusk's poetry collections include *Lake Studies: Meditations on Lake Champlain* (Lake Champlain Maritime Museum, 2011); the audio book *The Inland Sea: Reflections*; and *Kissing the Ground: New and Selected Poems* (Onion River Press, 1999). He lives in Vermont, USA with his wife, Irish expatriate and poet Angela Patten.

John MacKenna is the author of fifteen books – fiction, memoir, biography and poetry. His novel *Clare* will be republished in May 2014 in the New Island Irish Classics series, and his next novel, *Joseph*, will be published by New Island in September 2014.

John McAuliffe's third book, *Of All Places* (Gallery Press), was a Poetry Book Society Recommendation in 2011. He co-directs the Centre for New Writing at the University of Manchester.

Thomas McCarthy's first collection was *The First Convention* (Dolmen Press, 1978), and his latest book is *The Last Geraldine Officer* (Anvil Poetry, 2009). He has received the Patrick Kavanagh Award, the O'Shaughnessy Poetry Prize and the Ireland Funds Annual Literary Award. He works at the Frank O'Connor Library in Cork, and is a member of Aosdána.

Philip McDonagh has held a number of diplomatic posts, moving recently from Moscow to Vienna. His poetry has been published with the Dedalus Press, and in India, Russia, and in outlets such as the *Clifden Anthology* and the *Cork Literary Review*. His poem 'Anamnesis at Agrigento' is the basis of a musical cycle by Stanislav Prokudin, performed in the Kremlin in Moscow. 'Memories of an Ionian Diplomat' was performed this year with harpist Lily Neill in Vienna's Musikverein.

Allison McVety's first collection, *The Night Trotsky Came to Stay*, was shortlisted in 2008 for the Forward Prize for Best First Collection. Poems have been published in *The Times*, *Poetry London*, *Poetry Review* and *The Guardian*, and have been broadcast on BBC Radio 3. A second collection, *Miming Happiness* was published in 2010 by Smith/Doorstop, and a third, *Lighthouses* is due in 2014. In 2011 her poem *To the Lighthouse* won the National Poetry Competition.

**Fred Marchant** is the author of four books of poetry, the most recent of which is *The Looking House* (Graywolf Press, 2009). His first book, *Tipping Point*, won the 1993 Washington Prize from The Word Works, Inc., and a twentieth anniversary second edition has been recently published, with an introduction by Nick Flynn. He has co-translated (with Nguyen Ba Chung) *From a Corner of My Yard*, by Tran Dang Khoa, and edited *Another World Instead: The Early Poems of William Stafford, 1937-1947*. He is the Founding Director of the Creative Writing Program and the Poetry Centre, at Suffolk University in Boston.

**Garth Martens** won the 2011 Bronwen Wallace Award for Emerging Writers for the best Canadian writer under thirty-five. His first book, *Motive of Machinery*, will appear in 2014 from House of Anansi Press in Toronto. He was shortlisted in 2012 for the Bridport Prize, and in 2011 for the CBC Literary Awards. For the last eight years he has worked in construction on skyscrapers, hospitals and schools.

**Paula Meehan** was born in Dublin where she still lives. Recent collections include *Mysteries of the Home* (Dedalus Press, 2013) and *Painting Rain* (Carcanet Press, 2009). She is currently Ireland Professor of Poetry.

**Geraldine Mitchell** lives near Louisburgh in Co Mayo. Her second collection, *Of Birds and Bones*, was published by Arlen House in November 2013.

**Noel Monahan** has published five collections of poetry. His most recent publication is *Curve of the Moon*, published by Salmon Poetry, 2010. He has won several national literary awards for his poetry and drama. He is presently working on a *New and Selected Poems*, due for publication in 2014.

**Paul Muldoon**'s poetry awards include the Pulitzer and the T S Eliot Prizes. His latest book is *The Word on the Street: Rock Lyrics* (Faber and Faber, 2013).

**Richard Murphy** published his *Poems 1952-2012* this year with the Lilliput Press in Ireland and Bloodaxe Books in the UK, where *The Pleasure Ground: Poems 1952-2012* received the Summer 2013 'Special Commendation' from the Poetry Book Society. He also published with Lilliput an eBook edition of *The Kick: a Life among Writers*, containing historic photographs. Living in the central highlands of Sri Lanka for the past six years, he has designed a traditional Octagon, which village masons, carpenters and labourers have built on the brow of a tea garden. Richard's sister Mary (born ninety years ago in Ceylon) sponsored the work. The 'Murphy Octagon' will have many uses – writing, meditation, yoga, veena music, Kandyan dancing. It may also prolong the poet's Irish family connection with Ceylon and Sri Lanka, spanning more than 100 years.

**Kate Noakes** is a Welsh Academician who lives mainly in Paris, where she co-founded the literary association Paris Lit Up (**www.parislitup.com**). Her fourth collection of poetry, *I-spy and Shanty*, is forthcoming in 2014 from corrupt press.

**Billy Ramsell** holds the Chair of Ireland Bursary for 2013. He edits the Irish section of the Poetry International website, and recently judged the Shine Strong award for Best First Collection by an Irish poet at the Mountains to Sea dlr Book Festival. He has been invited to read his work at festivals and literary events around the world. His second collection, *The Architect's Dream of Winter*, will be published shortly by Dedalus Press.

**Rebecca Rogan**'s poetry has been published in periodicals in Ireland, England and the USA, including in *Poetry Ireland Review*, *Iota*, *Cobweb*, *The Honest Ulsterman*, *Kent Connections*, *Literary Mamma* and *The Same*. From 2010-2012 she was president of the Katonah Poetry Series planning committee.

**Biljana Scott** is a linguist and photographer, born in Geneva of Scottish-Slav parentage, and resident in Oxford for the last thirty years. She lectures in Chinese Linguistics at the University of Oxford and in Diplomatic Discourse at the London Academy of Diplomacy.

**Peter Sirr** has published several collections with Gallery Press, the most recent of which is *The Thing Is* (2009), for which he received the Michael Hartnett Award. He lives in Dublin and works as a freelance writer, editor and teacher. He is a member of Aosdána.

**Gerard Smyth**'s eighth collection is *The Fullness of Time: New and Selected Poems* (Dedalus Press, 2010). He won the O'Shaughnessy Poetry Award in 2012. He is a member of Aosdána and poetry editor of *The Irish Times*.

**Kenneth Steven**'s eleventh collection, *Coracle,* will appear in early 2014. He is first and foremost a poet, though he's also widely published as a writer of fiction and a translator from Norwegian. Each year he makes a number of programmes – most of these concerned with poetry – for BBC Radio. He lives in the heart of his native Highland Scotland.

**Matthew Sweeney**'s most recent collection is *Horse Music* (Bloodaxe Books, 2013). A retrospective selection, *The Night Post*, was published by Salt Publishing in 2010. *Death Comes for the Poets* (Muswell Press, 2012), a satirical thriller set in the world of contemporary poetry, was co-written with English poet John Hartley Williams, as was *Writing Poetry*, which was first published by Hodder in 1997 and has since been updated four times. He was Writer in Residence at UCC in 2012/13.

Mary Turley-McGrath's collection of poetry *New Grass under Snow* was published by Summer Palace Press in 2003. She was the winner of the inaugural Francis Ledwidge Award and the Annie Deeny Prize. In 2009 she was awarded an M.Phil in Creative Writing from Trinity College, Dublin. Her poems have been published in many magazines and anthologies, including *The Forward Anthology of Poetry* in 2011. Her second collection, *Forget the Lake*, was published in November 2013 by Arlen House.

Brian Turner is the author of the collections *Here, Bullet* (2007) and *Phantom Noise* (2010), both from Bloodaxe Books. He has received the Amy Lowell Travelling Fellowship, the US-Japan Friendship Commission grant, the Poets' Prize, and a Lannan Fellowship. His work has appeared on NPR, RTÉ, the BBC, and 'Newshour with Jim Lehrer'. A memoir, *My Life as a Foreign Country*, is forthcoming from Jonathan Cape in 2014. He directs the MFA program at Sierra Nevada College.

## Former editors of *Poetry Ireland Review*

| | |
|---|---|
| John Jordan 1–8 | Spring 1981–Autumn 1983 |
| Thomas McCarthy 9–12 | Winter 1983–Winter 1984 |
| Conleth Ellis and Rita E Kelly 13 | Spring 1985 |
| Terence Brown 14–17 | Autumn 1985–Autumn 1986 |
| Ciaran Cosgrove 18–19 | Spring 1987 |
| Dennis O'Driscoll 20–21 | Autumn 1987–Spring 1988 |
| John Ennis and Rory Brennan 22–23 | Summer 1988 |
| John Ennis 24–25 | Winter 1988–Spring 1989 |
| Micheal O'Siadhail 26–29 | Summer 1989–Summer 1990 |
| Máire Mhac an tSaoi 30–33 | Autumn 1990–Winter 1991 |
| Peter Denman 34–37 | Spring 1992–Winter 1992 |
| Pat Boran 38 | Summer 1993 |
| Seán Ó Cearnaigh 39 | Autumn 1993 |
| Pat Boran 40–42 | Winter 1993–Summer 1994 |
| Chris Agee 43–44 | Autumn/Winter 1994 |
| Moya Cannon 45–48 | Spring 1995–Winter 1995 |
| Liam Ó Muirthile 49 | Spring 1996 |
| Michael Longley 50 | Summer 1996 |
| Liam Ó Muirthile 51–52 | Autumn 1996–Spring 1997 |
| Frank Ormsby 53–56 | Summer 1997–Spring 1998 |
| Catherine Phil MacCarthy 57–60 | Summer 1998–Spring 1999 |
| Mark Roper 61–64 | Summer 1999– Spring 2000 |
| Biddy Jenkinson 65–68 | Summer 2000–Spring 2001 |
| Maurice Harmon 69–72 | Summer 2001–Spring 2002 |
| Michael Smith 73–75 | Summer 2002–Winter 2002 |
| Eva Bourke 76 | Spring/Summer 2003 |
| Peter Sirr 77–91 | Autumn 2003 / October 2007 |
| Eiléan Ní Chuilleanáin 92–95 | December 2007/October 2008 |
| Caitríona O'Reilly 96–99 | December 2008/October 2009 |
| Paul Muldoon 100 | March 2010 |
| Caitríona O'Reilly 101–104 | December 2007/October 2008 |